THE MONKEES

The REVERB series looks at the connections between music, artists and performers, musical cultures and places. It explores how our cultural and historical understanding of times and places may help us to appreciate a wide variety of music, and vice versa.

reverb-series.co.uk
SERIES EDITOR: JOHN SCANLAN

Already published

The Beatles in Hamburg
IAN INGLIS

Brazilian Jive: From Samba to Bossa and Rap
DAVID TREECE

Crooner: Singing from the Heart from Sinatra to Nas
ALEX COLES

Easy Riders, Rolling Stones: On the Road in America, from Delta Blues to '70s Rock
JOHN SCANLAN

Five Years Ahead of My Time: Garage Rock from the 1950s to the Present
SETH BOVEY

Gypsy Music: The Balkans and Beyond
ALAN ASHTON-SMITH

Heroes: David Bowie and Berlin
TOBIAS RÜTHER

Jimi Hendrix: Soundscapes
MARIE-PAULE MACDONALD

The Kinks: Songs of the Semi-Detached
MARK DOYLE

The Monkees: Made in Hollywood
TOM KEMPER

Neil Young: American Traveller
MARTIN HALLIWELL

Nick Drake: Dreaming England
NATHAN WISEMAN-TROWSE

Peter Gabriel: Global Citizen
PAUL HEGARTY

Remixology: Tracing the Dub Diaspora
PAUL SULLIVAN

Song Noir: Tom Waits and the Spirit of Los Angeles
ALEX HARVEY

Sting: From Northern Skies to Fields of Gold
PAUL CARR

Tango: Sex and Rhythm of the City
MIKE GONZALEZ AND MARIANELLA YANES

Van Halen: Exuberant California, Zen Rock'n'roll
JOHN SCANLAN

THE MONKEES

MADE IN HOLLYWOOD

TOM KEMPER

REAKTION BOOKS

For Alison, believer in dreamers

Published by Reaktion Books Ltd
Unit 32, Waterside
44–48 Wharf Road
London N1 7UX, UK
www.reaktionbooks.co.uk

First published 2023

Printed and bound in Great Britain by
TJ Books Ltd, Padstow, Cornwall

A catalogue record for this book is available from the British Library
ISBN 978 1 78914 707 0

Contents

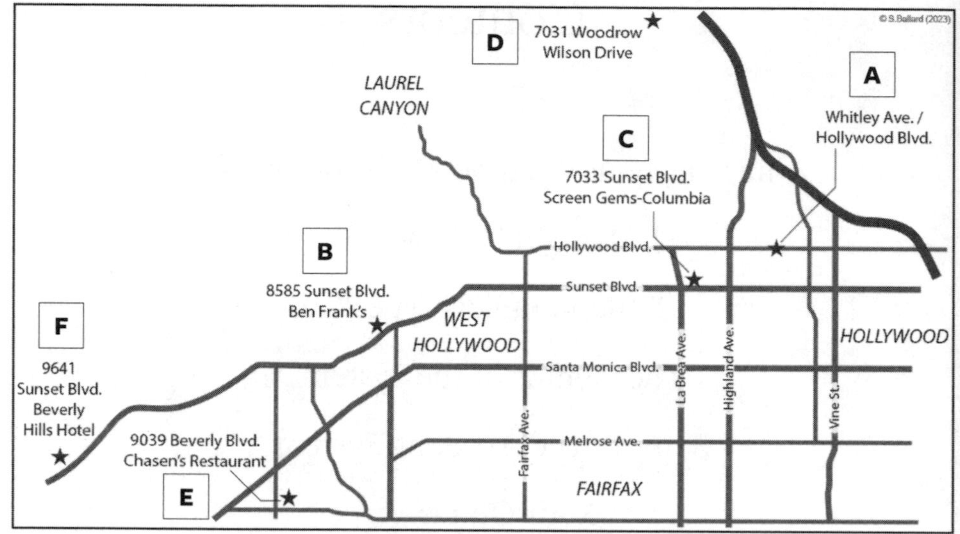

A. Chapter 1 – Intersection of Whitley and Hollywood Blvd.
B. Chapter 2 – 8585 Sunset Blvd., Ben Frank's
C. Chapter 3 – 7033 Sunset Blvd., Screen Gems-Columbia
D. Chapter 4 – 7031 Woodrow Wilson Drive
E. Chapter 5 – 9039 Beverly Blvd., Chasen's Restaurant
F. Chapter 6 – 9641 Sunset Blvd., Beverly Hills Hotel

Introduction: Machine-Made Monkees

In 1967, *Crawdaddy!*, the first magazine exclusively devoted to serious criticism of rock, declared with characteristically righteous conviction that the Monkees would "leave absolutely no mark on American music."[1] This prophecy followed a neutral accounting of the group's appalling commercial coups over the past six months: the band's "I'm a Believer" sold over 3 million units in America, making it the most successful single since "I Want to Hold Your Hand"; it moved 500,000 copies in five days in Britain (where fewer than two dozen singles a year cracked the 250,000 threshold), and their second album (released within four months of their debut) racked up 1.5 million advance orders. Moreover, studio musicians played all the instruments on these songs written by professional songwriters while the Monkees mimed the performances on their television show (they *did* sing on the records). Scandalized by the success of this pop group engineered by calculating corporate Hollywood executives (the joint enterprise of a television production company, a record company, and a music publishing business), *Crawdaddy!* bewailed the Monkees' profane triumph, taking some assurance in its sacral prediction that history would mete out justice against these false idols.

Yet over fifty years later, the Monkees remain unforgotten. This fabricated TV band pops up in almost every history of rock and pop, compelling the authors to reconcile, explain, and wrestle with its success, artistic and commercial. Every rock critic has felt the call to scrutinize the Monkees, to grapple with the problems they present, if not also to acknowledge the endurance of their songs. American music remains marked by the Monkees.

The Monkees represent a vital problem for rock and pop. Perhaps *the* primary question: is it the music that matters or the aura, the biography, the personality, and the image of the performers? Do we enjoy the art: delectably well-crafted songs, infectiously performed? Or do we need assurance of the central role of artists in creating the work?

Clearly, for millions of listeners, the primary roles played by other songwriters, producers, and studio musicians in the masquerade of the Monkees as a band remained of no concern. Nor did it alarm the casual listeners to the Top 40 or radio programmers who burnished their songs into hit after hit after hit in the late 1960s. That the Monkees relied on studio musicians and professional songwriters remains of little consideration to most contemporary listeners who recognize and consume "Daydream Believer," "Last Train to Clarksville," or "I'm a Believer" as bona fide pop classics.

A group put together through a casting call for a cheap television series depicting a fictional band that recorded hit songs on Top 40 radio seems easily dismissed, a short-shelf-life commodity, like a Campbell's soup version of the Beatles. And yet critics returned to the Monkees over and over like an obsession. Even fifty years later, the seminal and ambassadorial rock critic Richard Goldstein, who, with a small ensemble of peers, forged the template for rock scripture, actually distilled his essential imperative as a critic by framing it in an anxiety triggered by the prefab four: "I was haunted by the specter of the Monkees . . . The problem for me as a critic was distinguishing between Monkee wannabes and artists who had wrung a vision from their torment."[2] The very same industry that delivered the Beatles to him, his measure of true rock artistry, sponsored the Monkees. The intellectual struggle to balance the pleasures derived from the Monkees—the sonic satisfaction of shimmering melodies and sheer craftsmanship—with the aesthetic values informing his admiration of the Beatles testifies to the problem of the Monkees.

Why does it matter? The song, after all, does not change if we learn that someone else performed it, or parts of it; the effect of a guitar riff or drum fill remains the same whether Peter Tork or Micky Dolenz or a great studio musician laid down the track. Does it matter how the music originated? Does it matter how it all came together if you enjoy the song? It turns out the answer is mostly yes, at least for particular factions of rock culture. Rock or pop isn't solely about the music, then. By the time of the rise of the Monkees, critics, musicians, industry professionals, and a significant base of listeners subscribed to a rock mythos that established a set of values with *authenticity* at the top. The strict formalist, hewing to a concept of modernist purity of the medium, would claim that only the music mattered. But the rock mythos, while embracing values of modernity, harkened back at least and most vigorously to values of nineteenth-century Romanticism, where the artwork necessarily flowed from the vision of a singular genius.

The Monkees drew attention to the components of the industry necessary for any band or musician working in this commercial medium. They brought all the behind-the-scenes machinations of the pop industry—the publicists, the producers, the promoters, the studio musicians, the songwriters—onto the stage. The Monkees exposed why authenticity may not represent a legitimate issue at all. It's rather about how a system produces value, with "authenticity" at best a claim for only one strand within an organized system that includes other strains. The Monkees made the workings of the system explicit and yet produced value both playful and ironic, and authentically enjoyable. They winked at their own constructed nature and thereby at the constructive power of the system. The Monkees unveiled the monstrous machinery of pop and rock that operated even with its most allegedly authentic performers.

The campiness, irony, and pop energy of the Monkees project did not jibe with the emerging rock mythos. Just as the Monkees rolled off the pop assembly line, rock criticism—in newly formed journals like *Crawdaddy!* in 1966 or *Rolling Stone* in 1967, or new columns of criticism like Goldstein's in the *Village Voice*—began to explicate a mythology of the music. The criticism gained immediate strength and traction, drawn from the rock culture that had reified by the mid-1960s. Like all mythologies, the stories reinforced a set of original values: the myth of rock's rebellion, the myth of rock's underground, the myth of rock's origins in the blues, and, underlying all of these tales, the myth of rock's authenticity. That a mythos of such puritanical rectitude could develop around one of the most sophisticated, fast-paced, and complex mass media industries like the music biz, moreover at a time when its sales eclipsed $1 billion a year, remains a remarkable paradox. Yet the idea of authenticity has sustained an enduring component of the music industry to this very day.

At the same time as the debut of the Monkees, Andy Warhol and his Pop art cohorts signaled a modernity that questioned or overturned deeply held convictions about the artistic process by replicating industrial production techniques (and, in Warhol's case, hiring workers to aid in artistic production or using mechanical processes like silk-screening). In turn, intellectuals sensed a new cultural sensibility that matched this approach through an appreciation of irony and camp. By contrast, rock critics evaluated the products of the music business—commodities of completely networked commercial infrastructures built around industrial-scale production and distribution—by developing an aesthetics rooted in the previous century, heralding individualism in vision and artistic genius. The Monkees synched up with the strong commercial networks of Hollywood and tuned into the camp and Pop art spirit of the time, but they remained miles and centuries off when it came to rock's new intelligentsia.

But why not, instead, admire the Monkees for what they represent: a product of what André Bazin dubbed "the genius of the system," the cumulative result of an incredibly complex and cohesive organization of talented individuals, ranging from songwriters to studio musicians to producers—the system of Hollywood as an industrial operation and a real site. Bazin evoked the phrase in recognition of the conventions and artistic practices that came together, no matter the talent of the specific filmmakers, to create the great classical Hollywood films of the studio era.[3] The phrase applied to pop music as well, for it is no less a collaborative and industrial art form, and, in the case of the Monkees, one coincidentally rooted in Hollywood as a system and a place.

The Monkees developed out of the growing sophistication of the music business in Los Angeles as music publishers merged with production divisions and established a networked cluster of various interests operating to produce Top 40 hits. Recording studios grew as pop and rock spread across the radio dial and up the record charts, and relationships developed across the cityscape. Publishing companies hired songwriters and promoted their songs to the great maw of record companies, in turn feeding radio and retail.

Perhaps more than any other band, the Monkees demonstrate the cooperative networks supporting any artistic production. In his groundbreaking work *Art Worlds* (1982), the sociologist Howard Becker explicated how even the most individualized artists—say, a poet or a painter—rely on all sorts of collaborators and contributors. Artists of every caliber count on humdrum inputs from manufacturers of instruments and material—paper, canvas, paintbrushes, pens—to distributors—gallery owners, publishers, or bookstores—to more hands-on help, like the guidance of producers or editors. As a shorthand introduction to and illustration of his analysis, Becker offers the example of the great British novelist Anthony Trollope and his prodigious consumption of coffee as part of his early morning writing practice, arguing that Trollope's butler's barista skills played a role, therefore, in the production of his novels by providing a necessary boost of support to his prolific morning writing sessions. Such contributions to artistic practice range from seemingly incidental acts like coffee making or providing paper and ink supplies to copy-editing, formatting, and printing to the very last stages of artistic production, right down to the role of the audience. The great nineteenth-century Impressionist painters, for example, gained from the recent invention of tube paints, allowing them to bring paint out into the field, and even from the new network of trains, transporting them to the countryside for a painting's subject and allowing them to return to their Parisian studios by night. These support networks form around the needs and demands of artistic activities. Guitar sales and music shops, for example, experienced a significant uptick with the popular spread of rock in the mid-1960s. In consideration of the wide and necessary help artists drew on to complete even the most seemingly individualized works, Becker's research, rooted in sociological investigation and fieldwork, shattered many sacred myths about art, its process, and its practitioners. His expansive and inclusive world of artistic production worked against traditional Romantic conceptions of the artist as solitary genius. It did so, however, by bringing to light the incredibly social nature of all artistic practice.

Complementing Becker's perspective, the Monkees relied on the joint activity of all kinds of contributors. The Monkees represent a peculiar phenomenon as artists in an art world and its collaborative network, for they were created by joint activity; they were generated by their art world (the pop music industry) itself. The Monkees never existed as a band outside this world. An art world, its joint activity, put them together, and only then served them. Producers picked their music and managed their productions. Songwriters wrote their songs. Studio musicians performed their music. Individual Monkees only (at least initially) added vocal tracks. The Monkees performed as actors on the TV show. But, particularly on the initial musical side of the enterprise, it all came together through joint activity by practitioners in the LA pop music industry, creating the art through collaboration and coordination, almost without any central artist at all.

Artists working in the medium of rock or pop needed such a system. They needed it to reach their audience and to produce their end product: a record. Critics of rock like Charlie Gillett squirmed to make the industry—the business, the infrastructure, the manufacturing—fit a Romantic vision of the art form. In his early and intricate history of rock, *The Sound of the City* (1970), Gillett argued that independent record companies produced the most authentic, innovative, and influential records (tied to a regional vision, enhancing its alleged authenticity in his analysis), mapping Romanticism's valorization of the individual onto business practices. In doing so, Gillett resisted an examination of the system of support this business engineered for the very expression of the art form.

The dominant record companies like Columbia or RCA established platforms for artists to enact their vision. After all, every rock artist drew initial inspiration from listening to records. They needed the vast enterprise of such companies to materialize their inspiration and to garner any audience potentially interested in their work. A company like RCA set up the recording process, the manufacture of vinyl records, and their distribution. Each division of RCA developed a national infrastructure from their three major manufacturing plants to their national contracts with local distributors or their own setup in specific regions. These sides of their operations remained stable in the sense that marketing or manufacturing could respond to any developing trend. If accordian music suddenly became popular instead of rock or pop, that shift involved no changes at their record-processing plants. Machines for vinyl stayed the same, no matter what happened in between the grooves.[4]

Of course, the market for records changed all the time: ballads, songs about rebels, guitar rock, psychedelia, garage rock, girl groups, and so on. Critics like Gillett confused the turbulence of changing tastes with a lack of a system. Such a perspective misses out on the solidity of the system noted above, the enduring certainty of manufacturing, marketing, and the executive branches of the major record companies. The side of the business engaging with consumer tastes and fads in artistic expressions remained open to flux by design. It needed to respond, often rapidly, to changing tastes. Therefore, this side remained turbulent, dropping acts that failed to score with audiences, moving on as quickly as possible to new acts, all while attempting to sustain artists with some track record of hits (though even those artists remain susceptible to swift departures). The record companies knew that any record involves risk, so they kept that risk separate from their long-term assets like manufacturing plants or distribution divisions. Indeed, they often rented out those parts of their business to independent companies, who lacked such assets. A single record wouldn't sink the majors like it would—and did—for the many independent companies, which the majors tolerated for just that reason: they could survey the independents' risks on some artists and then snap up one who proved successful (a much cheaper operation than signing more artists to gamble on). On top of it all, companies like RCA owned a back catalog of previous hit records and enduring artists. When RCA took a gamble on the Monkees, for example, they had Elvis Presley in their back pocket, still selling like crazy in the 1960s and still moving his earlier records in retail stores.

When the Monkees came together through the machinations of major media players, such an engineered endeavor still could have flopped. RCA, their sponsoring record company, and their management team protected themselves, as with almost every deal in the business. First, some sense of protection came through in the expertise of advisors, through a series of gatekeepers who evaluate and advise the artists at different steps and stages of their artistic productions. Second, it came through the proven track records of musicians and songwriters (not always a guarantee, particularly with new artists). Most importantly, every company kept the costs of record production both relatively low (around $2,000 per song) and recoupable from the record's profits (which also meant, if it flopped, the company owed little or nothing to the artist, while if it succeeded on a major scale, both record company and artist got their share). Then, they released a whole slate of records, placing their bets wide on the table and, with the costs low on each, gambling that a few hits would make up for the minor but many losses. For every major label, this system worked. When the Monkees released their second single, for example, RCA put out 28 other records that month. Finally, the companies put artists on option contracts, meaning they had the option to drop them for poor performance but retain them for the contracted amount of time (a few years or, more likely, two or three promised albums).

Commercial rewards drove the system and provided the platform for artistic expression: that is, the making of a rock or pop record. A system of such complexity and commercialism, of course, created and even encouraged conflicts. Conflicts presented themselves in almost every corner. Scheduling the release of a record might conflict with the artistic desire to complete the work with more craft and perfection. Collaborators might be evaluated differently by band members, producers, and engineers (as well as record executives), ushering in protracted and unresolved debates over their skills. The goals of band members might not always align among themselves, let alone with their sponsors: the labels they worked for. Even in the case of the Monkees—a band created by the system—conflicts arose with surprising speed after their formation and ultimately splintered the enterprise.

Moreover, a system of such complexity like the recorded music industry lent itself to corruption, cheating, and nefarious contracts. Necromantic accounting made profits and royalties mysteriously disappear. Money ran away; esoteric clauses buried in contracts popped up later like bear traps, ensnaring artists to unforeseen obligations or ripping them off from anticipated profits. Even the Beatles and the Rolling Stones at the top, millionaires by any accounting, got famously fleeced by Allen Klein, a master manipulator of the system. Option contracts, wherein an artist could be dropped by a label over lack of sales, sound cruel, but they remained transparent at the very least and functioned as important mechanisms in the industry: a record label wouldn't take a chance on artists without such options.

The Monkees offered a transparent example of the industry's contractual relationships and its geographic relationships. Economic geography accounts for the Monkees. As economists going back to Alfred Marshall explain, business clusters and industrial districts fertilize new developments through the intensity and regularity of the transactions that reoccur in a tight space. In this case, the Hollywood origins fostered a joint venture between Screen Gems, the television division of Columbia Pictures, and RCA Victor, which distributed the albums. Screen Gems also owned a music publishing division which retained contracts with hitmaking songsmiths like Tommy Boyce and Bobby Hart, Barry Mann and Cynthia Weil, and Neil Diamond, who supplied songs for the Monkees. Great studio musicians like Louie Shelton, Larry Taylor, Glen Campbell, James Burton, and Billy Lewis aided the productions, as did top-notch recording engineers like Dave Hassinger and Hank Cicalo. With its ecosystem of specialized but complementary craftspeople and productions, an industrial town like Los Angeles could house and support such freelancing, cross-pollinating careers. Indeed, such activity sparked the rise of the Monkees.

The Monkees betray the tension between authenticity and industry, between the artists and the genius of the system. That system remained a network of social contacts within the urban grid of Los Angeles. We can, therefore, map out the concrete spatial relationships that contributed to efficiency and innovation in the production of a project and product like the Monkees. Appeals to traditional concepts like individual genius fail to explain them. The system, the city, and the geography of Hollywood and Los Angeles account for the Monkees.

1

Made in Hollywood

When Bobby Hart, originally from Arizona by way of a short gig in the army in San Francisco, arrived in Hollywood in 1958 in the hope of becoming a radio disc jockey (DJ), he walked the streets in search of opportunities. The promises of the Don Martin School of Radio drew Hart to Hollywood, as the school assured its students, in the bandwidth of ballyhoo, of surefire professional training and job prospects. Hart settled into an apartment on Whitley Avenue off Hollywood Boulevard, right in the hub of the city's emerging music industry.

Like most aspirants, Hart prowled the city for work. Turning down Santa Monica Boulevard one day, Hart hit a sign declaring simply but enticingly—for anyone like Hart infatuated with the recorded music business—"Record Labels, Inc.," and discovered that the shop printed labels for record companies like Specialty, Chess, Checker, Imperial, Era, Del-Fi, and other independents, mostly based in Los Angeles, all popping up with the advent of rock in the 1950s. Talking to the owner, Hart landed a job there, circling a little bit closer, it seemed, to the spinning vortex of rock and pop. On another expedition, Hart walked into a small recording studio, Fidelity Records, on Vine Street following its sign's invitation: "Come In & See What Your Voice Sounds Like—$10," another excursion within a 1–2 mile radius of his apartment. Entranced with the recording process, Hart dropped out of DJ school and started laying down recordings at Fidelity. Those led to a suggestion to see a record producer about his singing. So, Hart hit the streets again, walking the ten blocks down Sunset Boulevard to a producer's office in a quaint office mall of English-style houses called "Crossroads of the World." It turned out to be a career crossroads for Hart.

The producer, a bit of a small-time schemer like so many surfacing around this locational magnet to aspirants, offered to support Hart's production of a single 45 RPM record if he put up $400 to cover the recording costs. With this monetary layout (actually, a debt to the owner), Hart turned another corner, becoming a singer; the studio owner encouraged him to start developing his own material, so Hart became a songwriter too, with his first 45 stirring a little local radio buzz.

Hart's love of rock and pop had driven him to Los Angeles with the prospect of becoming a DJ, the only position he imagined he could fulfill as a teen in Arizona while daydreaming to the radio and pouring over the pages of pop magazines. Yet in the space and

Luring aspirants to Hollywood and capitalizing on the location.

encounters of his walkabouts, Hart transformed his ambitions and prospects, shifting his career with each new encounter, from DJ student to label-maker to singer and performer to songwriter, spinning his way into the central orbits of the Los Angeles music industry. Skip the needle ahead a few grooves to 1965 and we find Hart transformed into a professional songwriter with a stack of singles to his credit: "Lazy Elsie Molly" (recorded by Chubby Checker), "Come a Little Bit Closer" (charting at No. 3 for Jay and the Americans), "Peaches and Cream" (a hit for the Ikettes), and "Hurt So Bad" (a Top 10 hit for Little Anthony and the Imperials), among others, the latter hits written with his new partner, Tommy Boyce. In turn, the collaboration led the pair to a publisher and its vice-president Lester Sill, who would go on to work on the Monkees' productions, where Boyce and Hart would lead the pack of songwriters in the summer of 1966 as the TV show revved up its production schedule.[1]

Hart's story, and the corners he turned to end up on the Monkees' productions, reveal how much this mass media machine depended on a very concentrated local network of social and professional contacts. The Monkees project came together through major media companies: NBC purchased the TV show; RCA Victor handled the distribution for their record company, a division of Columbia Studios and their music publishing branch, with offices in New York and Hollywood. Yet this national media operation relied on the contingent and coincidental connections that occurred in the concrete space of Hollywood. When Hart met Boyce first in a recording studio and then in a publisher's office, an association that led to their writing and production work on the Monkees' first releases, it happened because the industry put local mechanisms—in this case, a recording studio and a publisher's office—in place.

A specific place: Hollywood. These mechanisms tied into a whole ecosystem of record companies, musicians, recording studios, and the milieu that fertilized creative types in clubs, restaurants, art galleries, and coffeehouses.

Making it in 1960s Hollywood: Boyce and Hart working on a song.

Like Hart, Tommy Boyce's love of music drew him to Hollywood, where he too tried out various roles as a back-up musician, performer, and occasional songwriter in his effort to score on the scene. The two eventual partners first met in a recording studio, the same one Hart started out in, when Boyce took lead vocals on some sample songs. Boyce had already logged time as a musician and counted a modest hit as one of his publications. Their paths crossed again in a publishing company's waiting room, and they soon got down to collaborating, hitting the ground running with the singles listed above.

No executive designed these encounters from the lofty perspective of some corporate office. Instead, the system networked them through local spaces organically developing in relation to one another—recording studios, song publishers, session musicians, producers, and engineers—as opportunities developed and expanded in this place known as Hollywood.

In this sense, mass media depends on very local brews. Locating a song publisher in this enriched environment, ripe with potential songwriters and performers, allows a company to find prospective artists through its proximity to the action, to lure in songwriters with an understanding of the latest trends picked up from nights at clubs or sessions with other musicians. Boyce and Hart dropped in regularly to their publisher's office to pitch their latest efforts or get a lead on the kinds of material big acts sought at any given moment.

The networked system of the industry put Boyce and Hart in place for the project that changed their fortunes. They didn't know it yet, but their song publishing company would get involved with a production enterprise synergizing the music and television industries in LA. This project involved creating a band for a weekly television situation comedy and simultaneously releasing recorded music under the band's name: the Monkees. The producers would put together the band of actors, then hire musicians and songwriters to release the music. The system eventually put this opportunity in front of Boyce and Hart, and they jumped at the chance.

When the Monkees' productions came together, when the management team sought out producers and song publishers for material to "play" the Monkees, recording engineers and studio musicians came together, many already in established local relationships with Boyce and Hart and others on the project. In this way, the Monkees relied and thrived on this highly localized ecosystem known as Hollywood.

The Los Angeles music industry in the 1960s grew out of the fields toiled and tilled by the movies, as did the expanding television industry in Hollywood sprouting up alongside its music business. As a location, Hollywood offered facilities and craftspeople whose specialties and skill sets readily and quickly adapted themselves to music. Recording engineers and studio musicians found steady work in the film and television business, and remained ready and waiting for the work offered by the recorded music industry. The city and industry also offered unions and guilds to manage, advise, and steer the technicians, craftspeople, and musicians that the growing recorded music business would rely on. A social and cultural world, vital to the recreational gossip and mingling of this creative hub, flourished in Hollywood as well, most spectacularly in the music venues, bars, and clubs on the Sunset Strip.

Capitol Records, the first label to spin out of Hollywood, percolated from the corner of Vine and Sunset, in the bright, big retail hub of Wallichs Music City, one of the first major stores specializing in record sales. It lured in customers far and wide, high and low, including stars like the songwriter Johnny Mercer (you must have heard “You Must Have Been a Beautiful Baby,” among his other hits), who got to know the store’s owner, Glenn Wallichs. When Mercer complained to Wallichs about the distribution of his own records, the two spun out the idea of their own label and pulled in Paramount Pictures producer Buddy DeSylva to form a partnership. Within a few years, Capitol ran with the majors, turning out hits like Mercer’s “Strip Polka,” “Cow-Cow Boogie” by the Freddie Slack Orchestra, Tex Ritter’s “(I Got Spurs That) Jingle Jangle Jingle,” and sensational new artists like Nat King Cole and Sammy Davis, Jr. Wallichs’s keen leadership focused on establishing a broad and robust distribution infrastructure (he knew the biz, after all) that could match the other leaders in the music industry. By the 1950s, Capitol added more hit artists like Gene Vincent and the innovative guitarist Les Paul, whose best-selling albums featured early experiments in overdubbing and multi-tracking. Then, in the early 1960s, they signed a local band: the Beach Boys. The world took notice. And so did their Hollywood neighbors.

MGM read the writing in the grooves and dropped a needle into it with their own label in 1946, scoring the initial film studio success in this new field. Frank Walker, hired as label head, immediately expanded the label beyond the logical and lucrative connection between the Hollywood studios and soundtrack records to also ensure attention to new popular styles like "hillbilly" and rhythm and blues. As he later told *Billboard*, "No record company is complete without country and western or rhythm and blues, or what we used to call race records." MGM's approach would typify the emerging record companies on the West Coast as they tuned in to the new sounds—namely, rock—as a competitive move to gain their grooves in the marketplace. In 1956, the Recording Industry Association of America (RIAA) reported that total record sales increased from $100 million to $331 million over that year. Moreover, this increase—43 percent in an industry that averaged about 4 percent increases annually—mostly came from independents and new music like R&B and rock and roll.

By now, all the major Hollywood studios heard the cash register tunes and circled into the disc business. Paramount Pictures purchased Dot Records in 1957 for $3 million, thereby acquiring Pat Boone, hovering just below Elvis in teen popularity. By the end of that year, United Artists, after failed bids on Imperial and Liberty records, stamped the United Artists Record Corporation, plugging records through their promotion division. By November, Columbia, 20th Century Fox and Warner Bros. all started shopping around for an independent label, courting Roulette, Imperial, Gee, Rama, Tico, Liberty, and Mercury, before starting their own.

The chart-spanning and head-spinning numbers of the recorded music business hooked Jack Warner on expansion, first unsuccessfully pursuing a purchase of Imperial, before committing wholesale to Warner Bros. Records in 1958. That same year Columbia Pictures—another spurned courter of Imperial Records—jumped into recorded music with the formation of Colpix Records (the name Columbia Records, of course, already having been taken by the East Coast major label). In tune with the other studio-backed record companies, Colpix announced an emphasis on the new forms of music, signaling a close reading of the sales charts and a commitment to novelty and new trends. Colpix's press agents broadcasted their plans to cover the jazz, pop, and rock'n'roll markets, stressing the fact that the label already dispatched scouts to Nashville.[2]

A bigger splash hit Capitol in the mid-1950s when the major British label EMI dropped out of the distribution deal they held with East Coast giant RCA Victor and bought up 96 percent of Capitol's stock. A tidal wave emerged out of this deal almost ten years later when Capitol incidentally got the U.S. rights to EMI's new act: meet the Beatles, America. On their own, the Fab Four quadrupled the West Coast label's sales.

Suddenly, LA became a veritable hit factory, spinning out one successful act after another in waves of different styles: rockabilly, R&B, its own distinctive surf-rock, and "folk and roll." Phil Spector became the first producer to win attention as something like a pop maestro (as famous as any conductor) for the "Wall of Sound" recordings he invented in LA, and they reverberated across the pop landscape like sonic seismic shakers. To achieve his wall of sound, Spector crammed timpani, multiple pianos, drum kits next to drum kits, trios of guitar players, and bassists into the small Hollywood Gold Star studios to record Wagnerian-transistor-radio pop symphonies like "Then He Kissed Me" or "Be My Baby." The drums burst through like fireworks or artillery, rattling the speakers, as the verses flooded over you with oceanic waves of densely layered instruments. Already stoking pop waves with the Beach Boys and set after crashing set of hits like "Surfin' Safari," "I Get Around," and "Catch a Wave," Brian Wilson felt the vibrations of "Be My Baby" as soon as he heard it on the radio. While driving down Sunset Boulevard one afternoon, the epic sound of this song by the Ronettes careened him to the side of the road. Reflecting on its artistry, he went home to write and arrange "Don't Worry Baby," and discovered the studio—often at Gold Star, like his hero Spector, or just down the block at United Western—as a new instrument to play. Laying tracks on top of other tracks, weaving in various instruments through the engineering of the recording process, he soon created his own masterpieces like "God Only Knows" and "Good Vibrations" for LA's own Capitol Records (an industry insider called the Beach Boys "the first Pop Art music").[3] Made in Hollywood. More precisely, made within a 1–2 mile radius within Hollywood.

Unlike New York's folk scene, which tended to honor older traditions of folk in form and lyrics, LA's folk performers proved far more adaptable to current times, with richer recording textures—echo chambers, for example, evoking space and depth in the choral singing—modern commentary in the lyrics, and more swinging beats and percussive accompaniment to back up the songs. Capitol led the surge with the Kingston Trio and the Lettermen. For example, 1965's folksy hit "California Dreamin'" by the Mamas and the Papas exploits the airy sounds of studio echo chambers to evoke a sense of depth and open space in the choral chiming of the vocal harmonies. The expansiveness of the singing rings through in the use of multi-track recording, layering call and response over one another as the echoing generates aural spatial dimensions. A snaking, hypnotic lushness coheres in the musical accompaniment, churned by the swinging reverberations of the rhythmic bassline, drums, and a swirling flute, carrying the song's sonic horizons well beyond traditional folk.

These regional artists drew from the soundscape all around them in 1960s LA. The Modern Folk Quartet on Warner Bros. Records, after working in more traditional folk in the early 1960s, moved on to the folk and rock fusion in their recording sessions (even working with Phil Spector). Sonny and Cher turned a Dylanesque phrase like "I Got You Babe" into a pop ditty, with lilting uplifting melodic lines delicately holding up the simple love-song lyrics. That same summer LA's the Turtles charted a Top 10 hit with a cover of Dylan's "It Ain't Me Babe"—the song that inspired Sonny Bono, no doubt—as the group shifted from surf-rock to "folk and roll." Jan and Dean, after scoring major hits in surf-rock and pop, even cut an album called *Folk 'n Roll* in 1965. And, of course, what started the "folk and roll" craze of 1965: the Byrds and their fusion of the Beatles and Dylan with their jingle-jangle cover of "Mr. Tambourine Man," echoed, in turn, by the Beatles, and the influence-jockeying occurring between the two bands (for example, Lennon's Dylanesque "You've Got to Hide Your Love Away" or "Nowhere Man," his mirror-house reflection on the Byrds' variation of the Beatles).

The "folk and roll" fusion of the Byrds reflected the spirit of innovation they (and everyone else) recognized in the Beatles. In this case, the LA quartet beat the Beatles to it. In terms of the region, the Byrds' folk-rock synthesis signified LA's receptiveness to new ideas, new forms, and innovation. The new artistic ideas matched the new experiments with the studio and recording equipment and drew innovators in all of these fields—studio engineers, songwriters, performers, and producers—to the city.

That innovation came out in subtle or less rarified forms as well. The great LA pop singer and songwriter Jackie DeShannon, for example, claimed that Jack Nitzsche's production work and the twangy treble he brought out on the 12-string electric guitars on her cuts "Needles and Pins" and "When You Walk in the Room," "really carved out a particular way of recording in LA," as both singles blueprinted the "folk and roll" sounds of the Byrds and, indeed, some early Monkees songs.[4]

The Beatles and the British Invasion resonated with the music coming out of LA because the moptops themselves echoed its pop topography: surf guitar's electric buzz (the opening slide on "I Want to Hold Your Hand," say, or the fuzzy riff on "I Feel Fine"), mixed with Chuck Berry-style R&B ("I Saw Her Standing There"), melded with harmonies echoing the Everly Brothers or girl-group choruses ("She Loves You"). The Beach Boys glistened with studio-perfected precision, layering their songs' point–counterpoint melodies, which reverberated through Beatles' tracks like "Here, There and Everywhere" and "Paperback Writer." At the very least, LA studio musicians and producers remained far more receptive to experimental new sounds than those on the East Coast. Phil Spector found the New York session players patronizing and conservative on his brief forays east, preferring the younger, hipper musicians back in LA.[5] Leading LA session musicians like Al Casey mocked the pedantic precisions and fussy formalism of New York session players.[6] Such innovation and creative energy in Hollywood, its receptiveness to new ideas and new artists, in turn, drew more artists to the city, more potential studio musicians, songwriters, and collaborators. Come together. And the beat goes on.

It made sense, then, in the context of the LA music scene and the impact of the Beatles, that the Monkees' producers sought out "folk and roll" and then mandated it to the project's various songwriters. Likewise, when Boyce and Hart took up their commission to supply songs for the Monkees project, they studied the sounds in the air, picking up on the "folk and roll" mixture characterizing the Beatles, the Dave Clark Five, and LA acts like the Byrds, Sonny and Cher, and the Turtles.

The British Invasion rattled the market even further. Performers acquired by the major labels just a few years earlier vanished from the charts. New firms—many of them newly sprouted in Los Angeles—jumped on the bandwagon, gaining from and contributing to a shake-up of the market. An early study of the 1960s pop charts by two sociologists revealed a significant increase in the number of new firms scoring hits.[7] That indicated that new fads and trends in music—basically spurred by rock and then the British Invasion—cracked the monopolistic dominance of the leading labels.

Splicing the numbers further, the data shows that many of the new acts sprang from Los Angeles. Rock shook up the establishment and opened doors for the new labels, a development that coincided with the rise of the LA music scene; even the East Coast labels signed up West Coast acts like the Byrds and Paul Revere and the Raiders. Thus, the numbers reveal a geographic shift in addition to a shake-up in monopolistic dominance. Indeed, in 1963, records produced in Los Angeles spent only three weeks at the No. 1 spot on the charts, compared to 26 weeks for New York-based recordings. By 1965, LA rocked twenty weeks at the top, with New York only landing one.[8]

The mixed-media industrial density of Los Angeles offered a rich feeding ground and ecosystem—film scores, television scores, television and radio advertising jingles, commercial music—for another of its musical species: the studio musician. Entrepreneurial creatures who got paid to play their instruments for a purpose, studio musicians provided accompaniment to singers on pop or jazz songs; contributed to the title songs for TV shows; played backup music on soundtracks for movies or television, or on jingles for soda pop or cereal commercials. Studio musicians ranged from professionals earning all their income from such work to others gliding through the occasional gig while pursuing songwriting or their own aspirations of an independent career.

It so happens that a young graduate student, Robert Faulkner, prowled around Los Angeles in this very moment—the 1960s rock explosion—gathering thick descriptions of the working life of these studio musicians, the subject of his eventual dissertation. Faulkner's research in the trenches revealed the significant role that social networks played in the career of an artist. He discovered that most of the work came to musicians through the informal contacts they made with one another and the reputations they built with other musicians. These led musicians to recommend each other for jobs as much as producers scoured sessions in search of accompanists. The Los Angeles area also offered a variety of work, making their practice more engaging and interesting as they could switch musical genres or purposes like doing jazz or classical or a soundtrack for a dramatic or comedic film or television.

Save for a handful with steady studio jobs, these musicians worked as guns for hire while belonging to the American Federation of Musicians (AFM), which regulated their minimum pay scales and working conditions. In the mid-1960s, the Los Angeles branch of the AFM held more than 18,000 members, ranging from pros who paid the bills through full-time work in the business to amateurs who only played occasionally. Some could sight-read a score on the fly, a skill that enhanced their reputations. Some specialized in techniques, like a good solo, or in genres. Some could play multiple instruments. At any rate, they had to be flexible and adaptable. Each project offered unique problems or issues: the particular artist, the melody or rhythm of the song, the balance or harmony. "This inherent variety in studio work," one insider explained, required "musicians to be prepared for uncertainty. They always have something new to play, someone new to play under, and they must be on top of their musical skills all the time."[9]

Based on their skills—their quick-reading eye, their creativity and command—a core group of a hundred or so musicians commandeered most of the elite jobs. These high-caliber musicians, steadily in demand by producers, composers, and artists, and other studio personnel could take home $20,000 to $80,000 a year.[10] They played for Sonny and Cher, the Beach Boys, Phil Spector, the Byrds, the Mamas and Papas, and, of course, the Monkees, the Los Angeles music scene offering them all a fertile landscape to sow.

The Monkees' productions banked on the availability of studio musicians and the speed at which they could be deployed in this region to execute recording sessions swiftly as the project gained momentum over the summer of 1966. It would not surprise Faulkner to learn how many of the studio musicians on the Monkees landed their jobs through their established social connections. Larry Taylor, the bassist on "Last Train to Clarksville" and the first two albums, illustrates the surprisingly overlapping networks lacing through this coveted inner circle. Before he reeled in the Monkees job, Taylor worked with major players like Terry Melcher, Bruce Johnston, and his older brother Mel, the drummer for the Ventures. He played on 1959's "Moon Dawg!" by the Gamblers, a Ventures-style twangy surf tune arranged by Nick Venet—arguably the first surf song—released on World Pacific Records, an LA label; it failed to chart nationally but became a big hit on LA's KFWB pop charts. Taylor also played a regular gig with a band, the Candy Store Prophets, headed up by Bobby Hart. Thus, when Hart got the green light in the summer of 1966 to begin producing material for the Monkees, Taylor got the call, joining his Candy Store bandmates Gerry McGee on guitar and Billy Lewis on drums. Along with the great session musician Louie Shelton and Wayne Erwin on guitars, they played on most of the Monkees' tracks laid down that summer, including the band's first single, "Last Train to Clarksville." One year later Taylor joined Canned Heat and moved on from his session work to a career with the band.

Hollywood was able to draw in all these studio musicians because it contained so many recording studios and, therefore, job opportunities in a concentrated space.[11] Recording studios sprouted up all over the city in tandem with many of the new record companies, but also to support the talent in the town. Popular crooners doubling as

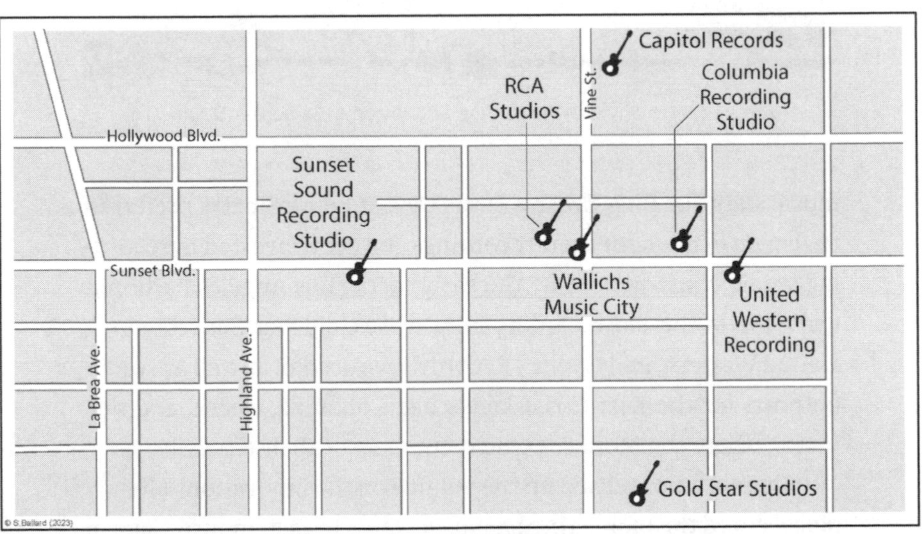

Compact disc business: Hollywood recording studios and record companies.

Monkee heart: RCA Victor Recording Studios on 6363 Sunset Boulevard, where most of the Monkees recordings took place.

movie stars like Bing Crosby, Doris Day, or Frank Sinatra preferred to remain in town for their recordings and even invested in recording studio construction. By the early 1960s, Los Angeles harbored major top-of-the-line recording studios like Gold Star, Sunset Sound, United Western, and Capitol Records' own studio, as well as studio outposts for the East Coast labels like Columbia, Decca, and RCA Victor, where the Monkees would cut most of their tracks.[12]

These studios turned up the volume on the innovations already plugged into the pioneering LA music scene. In fact, in 1956 Capitol Records, with the infusion of cash from its deal with EMI, constructed a state-of-the-art studio from the ground up, literally: "Studios A, B, and C" occupied the first floor of the company's striking new office tower at Hollywood and Vine. Innovative recording artists like Les Paul chipped in on the plans, with the trailblazing guitarist designing the studios' four shock-mounted echo chambers. Capitol's modernizations included using Ampex 200 tape machines, which allowed for multi-tracking and more dexterity in editing, acoustical techniques that offered more provisions for reverberation and greater separation in frequencies, among many other advances.[13]

Innovations like those informing the new Capitol studios charged through the city's circuited community of producers and recording engineers. Indeed, the latter group ran their own publications and conferences where they exchanged ideas on recording, studio layouts, absorption boards, isolation screens, directional and omnidirectional microphones, new strategies, and new technology. They shared a spirit of experimentation; the latest equipment and ideas matched the new buildings.

Bill Putnam led the pack of these influential engineers—Crosby and Sinatra bankrolled Putnam's creation of United Western studios—and he shared his ideas in conference presentations, mentorship, and simply leading by example: overdubbing multiple voices onto tape, mastering recordings at half-speed, using delay lines, mixing to create artificial reverb.[14] In the same spirit of updating recording studios, a former Disney recording director established Sunset Sound in 1962. It began as a place for recording Disney soundtracks and advertising jingles but soon became a major breeding ground for LA pop and rock, a spatial synecdoche of the pop music industry growing out of the film industry's bedrock.

From the mid-1960s, these establishments racked up hit after hit. Sunset Sound served up Love, the Turtles, the Doors, Buffalo Springfield, and Herb Alpert; the Beach Boys cut *Pet Sounds* and other classics at United Western, where the Mamas and the Papas and the Righteous Brothers made chart-busting records; Phil

Spector commandeered the knobs at Gold Star, recording hits by the Ronettes and the Righteous Brothers; RCA Studios in Hollywood hosted the Rolling Stones, Jefferson Airplane, and the Monkees.

The Monkees' recordings occurred in the heart of this vital activity, getting experienced musicians and engineers on board as a result of this density of resources and proximity of talent. A map of RCA Victor in relation to these major LA recording studios illustrates the incredible local concentration of these essential units of mass entertainment: RCA Victor at 6363 Sunset Blvd.; Gold Star at 6252 Santa Monica Blvd.; United Western at 6000 Sunset; and Sunset Sound at 6650 Sunset. An afternoon road trip would take you all of twelve minutes to cruise by each one, and you'd only log a bit over 2 miles on the odometer. Even a lesser facility like RCA Victor kept up with the competition through the trade of engineers and producers, who pushed the equipment and setup there—adding a four-track recorder, for example, then an eight-track, and so on—to match the standards established by the leading Hollywood studios. RCA's recording engineers included Dave Hassinger, who worked with the Rolling Stones at RCA Studios (he engineered not only "(I Can't Get No) Satisfaction," with its breakthrough use of the fuzz box, but the *Aftermath* sessions, and many others). Hassinger worked the console on much of the Monkees' first batch of recordings, with another experienced engineer, Hank Cicalo, spinning the knobs for their subsequent recordings. Both engineers came with experience from working relationships with leading engineers and producers like Jack Nitzsche, for example, and, by association, his work with Phil Spector. Information and innovation ran through their relationships like circuitry.

If the burgeoning Los Angeles pop music industry retained advantages in terms of its geography—growing within the fertile ground of Hollywood, with studio musicians, writers, and performers already percolating in its bedrock—it initially held a geographic disadvantage when it came to pop radio. LA remained just a little too far off the dial in the 1950s for its soundwaves to spark any significant influence or pulse. The eastern networks had long ago wired into the infrastructure and operations of the radio business, an empire of the airwaves difficult to surmount. And though LA radio hooked up to the powerful Top 40 format late in the game as well, when it finally did so in the 1960s, its stations jolted to a national amplitude—amplifying, and amplified by, the pop music explosion of the region. The Monkees bolted out of this bandwidth.

The Monkees represented a new television band, but they were just as much a radio band. Moreover, radio sustained very real visual dimensions. Radio interacted visually with its listeners through magazine tie-ins, billboards, posters, in-person appearances, and advertisements tied to its DJs and the pop stars they played. Radio sponsored local contests, hosted live at the events by their DJs, and also sponsored concerts, usually emceed by their DJs. Radio plastered main drags—like the Sunset Strip—with billboards featuring their logo, slogans, and pictures of their DJs, who also featured in print advertisements in local newspapers and magazines, if not their own radio-sponsored publications. Listeners could hear and *see* the DJs and the artists. And major radio stations published magazines with articles and pictures on the DJs and the latest pop music acts and news. LA's *KRLA Beat* may represent one of the first rock magazines for the quality of its writing and reviews.

KRLA started this four-page promotional giveaway publication in 1964, its title—"Beat"—riffing on the bandwagon of the Beatles and their sensational debut in the United States that year which bombarded the airwaves, TV, and radio with their songs and personas. A measure of the audience's desire to know more about the songs, the artists, and music culture in general, *KRLA Beat* evolved quickly from its initial four pages to doubling the page count within a year, and quadrupling it by 1966, when it grew into a dedicated rock magazine with journalistic articles, think pieces, news and reviews, distributed to local music stores and newsstands. When the Monkees debuted, the *Beat* featured extensive coverage of the band, as did every other radio promo paper.

Radio programming gained more importance in the late 1950s as actual radio sets in the United States increased by 30 percent over the decade. Cheap transistor radios charged the spike, and the portable, almost personalized aura of the device helped it play a huge role with teenagers, who could tune to their own stations and listen in privacy, away from the family, lacing their listening with an intimacy infusing the songs and the DJ's patter. Car radio promised a similar sense of individuality, offering control over your private mobile sonic space, all while the number of AM radio stations during the 1950s increased by 27 percent. Moreover, as the amount of radios proliferated in households, programming shifted to more discrete audiences, targeting different family members, age groups, and demographics. Programming changed over the course of the day—drive-time and after-school hours (time for teens to tune in) became key focus times—to reflect different groups of listeners or stations converted wholesale to programming that targeted specific groups, like teenagers.[15]

Designed to capitalize on novelty and repetition, Top 40 programming debuted in the early 1950s and expanded to a chain of Midwest radio stations before radiating rapidly across the country's airwaves. Nebraska's KOWH programming director, Todd Storz, stakes the strongest claim for originating the format, but the idea hovered in the air everywhere at the time. Whether or not the inspiration derived from a jukebox, where demand determined a record's staying power in the machine, or the habits of jukebox users to play a certain set of records over and over (as one origin story goes), the logic remains clear: patterns of popularity indicate play.[16] The Top 40 format took a set list of popular songs and repeated them all day long. It involved outlining a chart of the top requested songs (Top 40) and playing them on a schedule, a rotation that would feature the most popular songs at least three times in peak listening hours.

Forty songs roughly fit into a three-hour rotation, but some say that 40 approximated the typical number of 45s in a jukebox.

Most of the Top 40 determinants came from sales charts published in trade journals like *Radio and Records*, *Billboard*, *Cashbox*, and *Record World*. Those charts based rankings on record store surveys of sales or radio requests or a mixture of both, something of a circular measure and certainly not an exact science. The Top 40 chart then spun the major hits, slowly dropped those on the wane, and supported a few slots to test out or introduce new songs to the rotation. Top 40 built its approach around programming rather than the choices of individual DJs (they sometimes got a slot or two for their own choices and/or their own picks of potential hits). Jingles, news updates, traffic reports, and other features were designed to make Top 40 radio appeal to car listeners. The concept swept across the land. Storz consulted many stations directly, but stations also readily imitated the format on their own, checking for the hits in *Billboard* magazine and other playlists. The *Gavin Report*—a "tip sheet" in the parlance of the trade—illustrates how these different elements of the system worked together. For a modest subscription price, radio stations consulted the report, which itself consulted numerous radio stations for their tips, song picks, and recommendations. The trade magazines featured similar columns, all spreading the word through the industry.

KFWB, the first LA station to adopt a Top 40 format, picked it up in 1957, the decision of program director Chuck Blore, who dubbed it "Color Radio." This was a spin on the new color televisions hitting the market, an association that connotated modernity, novelty, and a visualization of sound. This programming switch shifted the station from its previous "mish-mash" of song cycles to an orientation around pop, rock, and R&B—and spunky DJs. Blore's success helped to channel the Top 40 style to other stations.[17] Blore defended his style, where the Top 40 dictated music choices, rather than the DJ, arguing that the format made the typical DJ "a better DJ. He no longer is permitted to run off at the mouth, but he is encouraged to assert his personality. He may not be as free to inflict his musical tastes on the public, but now, and rightfully," Blore claimed, referring specifically to the sales charts, "the public dictates the popular music of the day."[18]

Down the dial and over the hill, Pasadena's KRLA challenged KFWB when it too switched to a Top 40 format one year later. But the biggest shake-up in Los Angeles came when Bill Drake and Ron Jacobs transformed the Top 40 format at KHJ in 1965, quickly making the AM station a pop radio market leader. Once Jacobs made the managerial decision to switch formats, the programmers kickstarted the new direction by immediately running out and grabbing a KRLA song list from Wallichs Music City and two copies of all the records on the list. Shortened to a thirty-title current rotation, they started with this variation on the KRLA list and called it Boss Radio.[19]

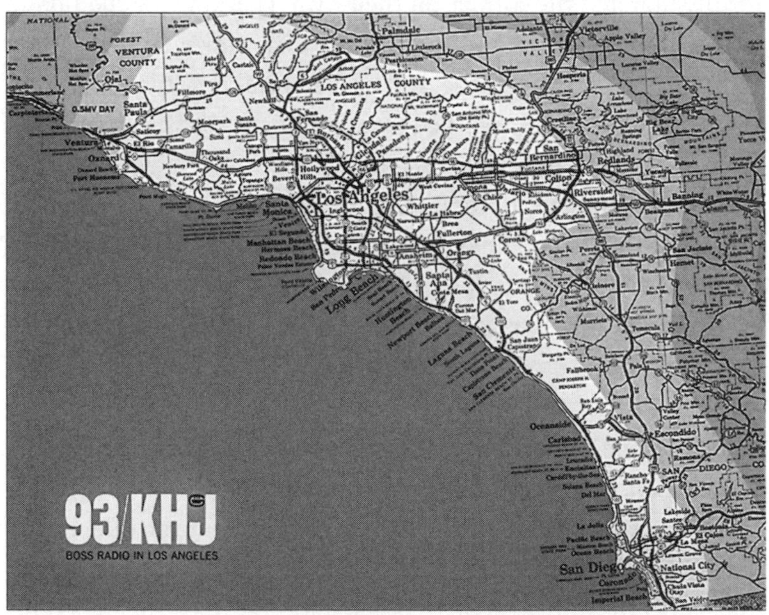

KHJ's transmission coverage map reveals its extensive reach beyond Los Angeles, though its influence radiated even further across the country and the music industry.

In addition to shrinking the Top 40 to a Top 30, they honed DJ talk to quick patter—ossifying the clichéd hyped-up pitch of DJs—and bursts of news flashes. Otherwise, nothing but music, with a new song every two or three minutes. Their Top 40 format limited commercials to about twelve minutes per hour. They allowed for about four hundred oldies (pop and rock from the late 1950s and early '60s) to mix in the song chart, "goldens" as they called them. A song from only a year earlier qualified as a "golden"—taste moved fast—along with some select 1950s classics.

The imperative kept everything upbeat and fast-moving with no lags. Cut the chatter down and make it speedy. Add catchy jingles to make people remember the station they tuned in to. To this end, KHJ even hired Bruce Johnston (from the Beach Boys touring band) and Terry Melcher (the lightning hot local producer of the Byrds and Paul Revere and the Raiders) to create and sing one of the station's jingles: "It's the new KHJ/ You don't know what we've got/ While Los Angeles goes, now/ It goes all the way/ And we know that you'll go/ For the KHJ/ It's the sound of success/ Boss Radio, in LA—KHJ."[20]

Even if music played the dominant sonic role, the DJs needed distinctive personalities pitched in popped-up peppy seconds. The patter remained both highly stylized according to the individual on-air personalities—most of whom picked up nicknames (Charlie Tuna, the Real Don Steele, the Big Kahuna) that were then featured in the station's billboards, advertising, and pamphlets—and predictable: "Boss Radio . . . handing you the heavy hits, around the clock . . . where the hits happen first . . . the hits keep on coming!"[21]

The "Real Don Steele" typified the approach, with performative zingers and patented patter hopped up in high decibels: "I got nothing but groovy, those groovy golds. We're gonna kick it out here on a fractious Friday. Jumbo city! Take a trip!"[22] Each DJ performed their own shtick—a tradition but again finely honed and whittled down at KHJ in bursts of energy. The program director held regular "jock

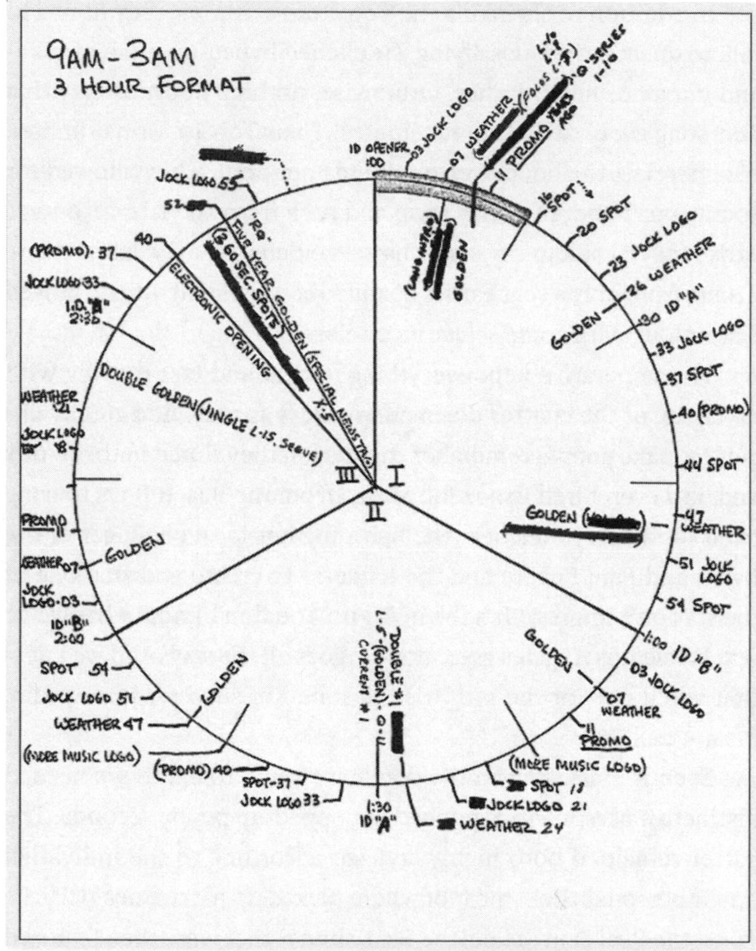

Wheel of fortune: a Top 40 Wheel from KHJ reveals the thin chances of slipping in a new single to the rotation.

meetings" with all the DJs, finessing their approach, reviewing new ideas, and parsing the logic of their playlists.

Memo after memo, sometimes daily, in KHJ's internal files insist on keeping the energy level hyped up, spewing out notes on everything from a DJ's use of slang, the speed of their delivery, the timing of fade-ins or fade-outs, the pairing of songs, the timbre of their voices, the sense of clever spunk in their patter, their song sequences, and their playlists. An April 7, 1967, memo, for example, notes that "it is uncool to: . . . use the word 'psychedelic' on the air (unless written into spot copy). Rapidly falling out of favor with whoever it is who's 'in.'"[23] Another circulated internal document drew from a survey to inform and report on the latest slang: "A gas . . . bitchen . . . boss banana . . . freaky . . . hubba hubba . . . out of sight . . . phoikeadelic . . . raspy . . . zunzabah." Words of wisdom.

Ruling over the DJ's spinning turntable was the "Drake clock," a circle with a circumference segmented according to a regulated pattern: an upcoming hit here, followed by certified Top 40 singles, with a "golden" here and there. More exactly, at the top of the hour, a single blasted through the speakers; about three minutes later, DJ patter and a commercial break; seven minutes later, another single, followed by more songs and a quick news review. Spots followed a numerical sequence: "3-7-11-16-20 . . . 30-33-37," and so forth. The program director picked potential hit singles to sample in and out of the clock by the DJ and carefully monitored the DJs in their allegiance to the clock's patterns.

In an August 17, 1967, memo to his KHJ DJs, Ron Jacobs, always fine-tuning, broke down the wheel or clock into the following pattern:

> 2 Boss 30
> 1 Hitbound
> 2 Boss 30
> 1 LP track
> 2 Boss 30
> 1 Hitbound, etc etc.
> OK to come off news and ID's with LP track if it's big & *up-tempo*.

Note the limited slots for singles deemed "Hitbound." The Top 40 format at KHJ, as elsewhere, meant that breaking a new record remained within impossibly narrow odds.[24] A DJ rotated through songs already charted—in other words, racking up sales on record store lists and primarily the *Billboard* charts—or already proven hits like the "goldens." With maybe one, three or five open programming slots on any week, fifty or more new singles vied for entry. In fact, a 1963 *Billboard* survey revealed that only 23.7 percent of received singles got played more than once, while over 60 percent never got played at all by radio programmers.[25]

In many ways, the concept solidified the immediate hook in the intro to pop songs and their formal structure, moving quickly, for example, from the verse to the catchy chorus: "(I Can't Get No) Satisfaction," "96 Tears," "I Feel Fine," "You Really Got Me," hook after hook after hook, perfectly sharply honed to slice into a slot on the Top 40 wheel. Songwriters, producers, and record companies absorbed this logic, knowing fully well that most DJs spun a 45 for about four measures before discarding it as they selected potential add-ons for their programming from the weekly stacks of singles submitted to them.

Drake and Jacobs claimed that "momentum" offered one of the factors of evaluation in considering additions to their playlist. Such an intangible concept becomes more tangible when you clear away the ambiguity and read the code. Momentum meant a particular song supported by big promotion by the record company or an artist with a proven track record. A radio programmer might find more comfort in gambling on a single knowing that wider promotion backed the decision, all the while retaining the option of dropping the record if it failed on its first few cycles of airplay.

KHJ's influence extended beyond their coverage area since, by the mid-1960s, Los Angeles had established itself as a leading center in the pop music business. By then, KHJ captured national media coverage of their own influence, with *Time* magazine running a piece on their powerful programmer and *Esquire* claiming LA rock radio represented the best in the country.[26] Moreover, the trade papers like *Billboard* and tip sheets like the *Gavin Report* scrutinized and reported on trends and developments in KHJ's programming.[27] As a *Gavin Report* at the end of 1966 noted, "KHJ-Los Angeles is probably the most monitored and air-checked station in the U.S. today."[28]

As much as any component of the pop and rock music industry, radio illustrates its systematic structure. Radio operated outside of the actual creation of music, serving only as a platform for the appreciation, promotion, and reception of the art form. Yet the art form relied on this relationship as record companies needed radio for promotion and sales. The two parts of the system brokered a deal: free airplay in exchange for promotion, if and only if a record made the cut. As one executive explained clearly: "Airplay is the lifeline of a company."[29] In turn, radio stations relied on hit records to boost their audience, their ratings, and their appeal to advertisers. KHJ, for example, developed an elaborate promotional campaign around the Monkees' first release because they stood to gain in isolating a Top 40 hit early and repeatedly by tapping into its audience (and heightening their ratings and advertising rates). All the members circuited through the system governing the production, release, and promotion of the Monkees' first single sought an instrumental role in making it a Top 40 hit. If it proved successful, the system would reward them all monetarily and reputationally for the role they played in its success.

Take one song, the Monkees' first release, "Last Train to Clarksville," as an illustration of the inputs of all these different aspects of the system. When the 45 shipped on August 16, 1966, it sprang from the system's various gears and levers kicking in like clockwork:

> Songwriters: the management team activated a search from songwriters contracted with their publishing division for the right pop songs to lead with for the band's debut. Boyce and Hart got ahead of the pack of writers and landed a number of potential songs for consideration.

Producers: the recordings required producers to manage the musicians, make decisions on recording procedures, instrumentation, and the mixing. After a series of tryouts and stumbles, Boyce and Hart won the job on several early tracks, with other producers entering to cover additional material.

Recording studios: NBC greenlit the Monkees project for television and owned RCA Victor, who owned their own Hollywood recording studios, where most of the recordings took place.

Recording engineers: RCA Victor employed experienced engineers like Dave Hassinger and Hank Cicalo to assist the recording and mixing.

Studio musicians: since the Monkees, to greater and lesser degrees, remained relative amateurs as musicians, the management team and producers hired a string of studio musicians to record all the instruments and background vocals on the early tracks. The producers cycled in different Monkees to supply lead vocals on the tracks.

Radio: RCA's promotion department steered the distribution of the records and their promotion to major radio stations.

The management team plucked "Clarksville" as the band's debut single from a slew of tracks recorded over that summer. Boyce and Hart persuaded the team of their capacity not only to develop a bundle of songs but to steer their recordings through as producers, taking over the control room for most of the major tracks. Between July and October 1966, Boyce and Hart unspooled tapes for over 25 songs, enough for the twelve tracks on the first album and another dozen primed for follow-up releases. These included "Valleri," "Words," "She" (all released as later recordings), and cuts making the first album like "I Wanna Be Free," "(Theme from) The Monkees," "Take a Giant Step," and "Last Train to Clarksville." Some tunes from these summer sessions in remixed or reproduced form got released over two years later.

Astute students of their craft, Boyce and Hart recognized the eclectic range of songs on Beatles albums and sought to deliver a similar spectrum to the Monkees. "I Wanna Be Free," a ballad with strings, matched "Yesterday" in tone though the album cut charted on many Top 40 stations. "Gonna Buy Me a Dog" cued up the comedic tone of a "Yellow Submarine" (echoing its sound effects and silly banter as well) or the goofy charm of "Act Naturally." Boyce and Hart considered the gray, lonely, and spare "Mr. Webster" (another saved for a later release) their answer to "Eleanor Rigby." Other cuts ranged from mild rockers like "Let's Dance On" and "Tomorrow's Gonna Be Another Day" to garage rock ravers like "(I'm Not Your) Steppin' Stone."

"Clarksville" developed a melodic lyrical line in its verse over a single chord, jumping to a very Beatlesque 7th. The jangling guitars and rising, swirling harmonies matched LA's folk and roll sounds, with a strong flavoring of the Byrds and the Beach Boys (the lilting doo-wop break). It captured LA's own reception of the British Invasion with a rollicking hand-clapping steady beat like "The Last Time" by the Rolling Stones, "Party Line" by the Kinks or the Beatles' "Run for Your Life" (to which it likely owed its guitar hook).

Determined in their mission to bank enough material to survey for possible release, Boyce and Hart produced a few tracks by other songwriters on the team as well—Carole King and Gerry Goffin—and Monkee Michael Nesmith even produced a few of his own compositions. Boyce and Hart tackled a recording of "I'll Be True To You" by Gerry Goffin and Russ Titelman, a tune that had been lying around the song publisher's office since the previous year, if not earlier. The Hollies turned it into a UK hit that year (under the title "Yes I Will"), returning the tune to its British Invasion inspiration (the writers riffed on "If I Fell" after seeing *A Hard Day's Night*). Boyce and Hart and their team of studio musicians treated it to a Beatles vibe with a steady beat, plucking and strumming the chords, layering a soft harmony under the lead vocals by Davy Jones. "Take a Giant Step" came from the songwriting duo King and Goffin.

That same July afternoon Boyce and Hart taped versions of or additional tracks on five other songs: "This Just Doesn't Seem to Be My Day," "Let's Dance On," "(Theme from) The Monkees," "Take a Giant Step," and "Saturday's Child," songs that all made it onto the first album, as did "I'll Be True To You." Nesmith produced a few tunes, including his own rocking composition "Mary, Mary" (covered by the Paul Butterfield Blues Band), a track featuring top session players like Hal Blaine, Glen Campbell, Larry Knechtel, and others—another one vaulted for their second album. Most of the recordings took place at RCA Studios, with additional time logged at United Western Recorders' a few blocks down.

Recording sessions went on all day and often into the night (the AFM monitored overtime payments, a welcome increase for most of the musicians). Night work most often developed around the availability of various Monkees for their lead vocal tracks, though typically they recorded these on their own, on separate tracks from those with the studio musicians. In gathering and evaluating the material, the producers and songwriters worked together, weighing the success of the various recordings and their promise.

In its recording quality and overall mix, "Clarksville" stands out from many of the tracks logged that summer. The mix foregrounds the crisp twang of Louie Shelton's trebly bass string riff on his Fender Telecaster with just the right cackling reverberation emanating on the sustained notes through his Fender Super Reverb amp. The track sparkles most distinctively in the way the mix matches the high ring of the cymbals and the rippling arpeggios of the electric guitar.

RCA's recording engineer Dave Hassinger exploited the studio's collection of high-quality microphones on "Clarksville," pitching the hi-hat upfront in the production, adjusting the guitars at a high treble, and pinpointing their terrific plucking. Consider Hassinger's thoughtful reflections on miking a drumkit:

> I would always place the mics on everything myself. On the drums I would use overhead a German M-49 mic, a snare mic; some sort of condenser mic, but a lot of the time I would use the overhead to capture the sound of the snare . . . sometimes I would put on the hi-hat, a Shure, something like that.[30]

The careful calibration Hassinger describes here, dotting the drum kit with targeted microphones, splashes through on "Clarksville," with its sharp, snappy kick of the snare and the chiming cymbals. Hassinger manually controlled the volume knob on the mic covering the hi-hat as it chimed through on "Clarksville," hissing on every fourth beat with a sense of resolve and release.[31] The guitars jangle like the Byrds or Nitzsche's work on "Needles and Pins." It sounds like mid-1960s LA pop-rock through and through. Hassinger reserved Micky Dolenz's lead vocals (the sole Monkee on the track, by design) for a separate track and exploited the close miking to capture his wispy breaths, dramatic resignations that truly flavor the song with meaning.

"Clarksville" represents one of the best records released by the Candy Store Prophets. It hit retail shelves and record stores as a Monkees production, with the TV band on the cover and advertising. Moreover, the TV band mimed their way through performances of the song on the first season's early episodes, weekly national exposure that energized its quick ascent up the charts. But the Candy Store Prophets strummed its glistening waves on guitar strings, the snappy bass string riff and bass guitar licks, and the infectious hop-skip drums and cymbals. These studio musicians—Gerry McGee, Larry Taylor, and Billy Lewis—snared this prime job because they regularly gigged (up to six nights a week) with Bobby Hart at The Swinger, a club on Pico Boulevard, under the name the Candy Store Prophets (session musician Shelton joined them on the Monkees' tracks). Hart tried out songs with McGee, Taylor, and Lewis at the club, running through "She," "Words," and "(I'm Not Your) Steppin' Stone." Other leading studio musicians put in hours on more recordings for the band. Shelton contributed to over twenty tracks; the great drummer Hal Blaine logged over fifteen, guitarist Glen Campbell clocked over a dozen, and the same for bassist Larry Knechtel.

At the end of this productive summer, on July 31, the Monkees' management team held a listening session and picked "Clarksville" as the lead single, an exemplary and promising specimen of the "folk and roll" sound they sought from the start. This same session singled out the song selections for their first album. Then the recordings went straight to RCA's manufacturing division. With the single moving through the factory line, it came time to canvass the radio stations, priming them for its release. The Monkees' record company had RCA's experienced sales staff, with their national infrastructure of distribution and promotion, at their disposal. The parent company supplied them with 75 promo men to push their new single to radio stations across the nation. In Los Angeles, the television production company behind the Monkees machine collaborated with KHJ on an elaborate promotional campaign, a specialty of the hype-laden station, which often sponsored contests involving Los Angeles locations (they had featured TV's Batmobile in a recent campaign). This deal happened eight weeks ahead of the network premiere of the show.

An internal KHJ memo acknowledged the successful pitch with the Monkees' management and outlined their plan:

> Let's make a *real* "Last Train to Clarksville." We'll fill it full of KHJ Boss Radio "Meet the Monkees" contest winners. The Boss Jocks will be aboard doing live radio reports. And—here's the part that will blow everyone's minds—the Monkees will be along for the ride . . .

> We start playing the hell out of "Last Train" right now. KRLA will jump on the record talking up "The Last Train to Clarksville." They'll be promoting the next big KHJ promotion.[32]

Playing the hell out of "Last Train." That's the deal. Pushing this promotion played into KHJ prioritizing the single, and, at least until the "Clarksville" event transpired, helped to promote their own promotional event. If the single tanked after that, the station would drop it from its playlist.

KHJ then scrambled to find a small town nearby with a train station and one near enough to a public space for a crowd, a performance, and refreshments. They persuaded the Southern California town of Del Mar—an afternoon's train ride from Los Angeles—to rename the station and city for a day and host the festivities. Convincing listeners to jump on a train to support an unknown band and an unheard song entailed KHJ offering a contest for free

The bandwidth bandwagon: joint promotion with a local station lures listeners to take a chance on the Monkees.

color televisions for four of the participants, and KHJ packed a single train car with listeners. A few helicopters brought the Monkees to Del Mar, and they rode back on the train with 550 guests, playing a makeshift live set with the instruments at hand, the din of the crowd and train, no doubt, overwhelming the din of the amateur musicianship. KHJ filmed the event and spliced the footage together for their first Boss Radio TV Special on a local station.

The "Clarksville" event offered a typical way to get around the issue of payola, the recently outlawed practice where a record company directly paid a station to play a record. Here the promotional and commercial benefits remain mutual: that is, KHJ gains from the hype, the audience response, and the publicity. But the publicity stunt also serves the Monkees in promoting the new act, song, and show. Moreover, by tying the event directly to a radio station—sponsored concerts or ticket giveaways work in the same fashion—it encourages that station to continually mention the band and play their material (probably more frequently than they might with an unsponsored, ordinary new single). In other words, it effectively works like payola without any transactional evidence. The band lends their name and novelty to the station for hype, and the station lends their services to the band in exchange. The Monkees project doled out their brand to other stations as part of their campaign. KFWB, for example, received a visit from the band, as did a handful of stations across the country. They sent their Monkeemobile—a custom hot rod with the band's logo emblazoned on the doors—to the KFXM Inland Empire Custom Car Fair.

The backing of a TV show and major companies (NBC and RCA Victor, respectively) injected the Monkees with what KHJ's Drake called "momentum"; KHJ's risk in playing their single and joining in the promotion would be minimized by the broader support. Momentum represented one of the factors—aside from a previous track record of hits—needed to cut in line as a potential "Top 40 hitbound." The advertising in magazines and promotion in articles

Local news: exclusive programs enhance the radio station's reputation as well as the artists'.

and TV commercials bolstered the promotional campaign that KHJ joined.

Encouraged by the success of the "Clarksville" event—and the success of the single, no doubt—KHJ continued to promote the Monkees into the new year. In 1967 the station offered, as a January 13 internal memo instructs to its DJs:

> hourly Monkee feeds. All of these will come in on Boss Like #2 and be tape-recorded in advance. It is up to you to put that hour's report in the best sequence. Obviously, the best sequence is one where there are no spots (or following a 10-sec spot). *Never* use a Morgan-Monkee feed in the :19 slot.
>
> Your intro to him each time should be . . . "What's happening with The Monkees."

The memo explained that Robert Morgan would record his interviews and mini audio documentaries on the Monkees' activities on short, taped intervals for the DJs to insert into their programs, with tips on integration into their programming: "Morgan's end cue will be . . . 'This is Boss Jock Robert W. Morgan on the move with The Monkees.'" All this business with Morgan's Monkee exclusives also meant that the band would get more attention and airplay on the station. To pump up KHJ's own exclusive access—or seemingly exclusive (other stations received their own deals)—to the Monkees only encouraged more airplay of the Monkees' songs, since getting more songs in circulation enhanced the alleged exclusivity of the station's access to the band. In fact, a KHJ internal memo to the DJs reminded them of this bargain:

> Since there are five Monkee songs on the list, you should be able to follow each Morgan-Monkee feed with a rotating Monkee song. This means:
>
> (a) Feeds should be in sequence prior to a current record (except for "Clarksville," which will be in this weekend's Golden Book and is okay to use following a feed.)
>
> (b) You should hold your Monkee song until it can be used to follow a feed.
>
> Once you know Morgan's tape for the hour is available, be sure to plug ahead like crazy! If you have any idea of what's on the tape you can be more specific in your plug ("Robert W. Morgan chats with David Jones backstage in Cleveland, upcoming on __________ Show.")
>
> Morgan, for overnight Saturday and Monday morning through 9am, will pre-tape a bunch and they will be slated for the hour in which they are to be used.

The memo clearly points out that KHJ's hype for the Monkees enhances their own special promotion—Morgan with the Monkees and vice-versa. In turn, the memo instructs every DJ to play at least one Monkees song every hour. Also note that "Clarksville" already qualifies as a "Golden" less than six months after its release.

The relationship to radio remained so strong that the band's management asked KHJ—and probably other stations—to run interference on some early static surfacing around the group and the project. A KHJ memo from November 29, 1966, revealed that the Monkees were already getting flak for their manufactured media machinations:

> When you can please talk positively about the Monkees . . . if you say anything. Backplug all their records have been World Premiered on KHJ . . . talk about Clarksville . . . and refer to their TV show as a "smash." This last point I mention because their producer called bugged about jocks on other stations putting down the Monkees and hinting the series might be cancelled. Nothing could be further from the truth . . . the ratings are good and there's 100% sponsorship. So . . . if you do talk about them, make it positive.

KHJ stuck with the Monkees because the numbers told them to. Part of KHJ's system of operations involved polling teenagers at local events. One such survey in 1966 revealed that 361 of the polled teens (out of about 1,000) picked the Monkees as their favorite group, with the Stones nabbing 258 votes, and the Beatles, surprisingly, only 75. The Monkees led the pack on "favorite new group (last six months)" as well: 445 voting for them, with second place (113 votes) going to the Seeds. Their survey also revealed that 637 respondents voted KHJ as their favorite station, with KRLA clocking a distant 215.

Tip sheets tuned in to LA's leading Top 40 station, highlighting the success of "Clarksville"; the *Gavin Report* picked the single early on as a "Hot Shot" and then as "Smash of the Week" in its October 7, 1966, issue, noting: "In some cities it's already charted #1." It further noted that the flip side ("Giant Steps") was also pulling good phone response and the TV show's theme song is "one of the hottest request items now being played." As predicted by the *Gavin Report*, within a few months after its release, "Clarksville" stationed itself at the No. 1 spot on *Billboard*'s Hot 100.

Louie Shelton's session work as a guitarist on "Last Train to Clarksville" encapsulates the entire system at play here. In the recording studio, Shelton jammed through the music sheets like a pro. But he understood—as did everyone in the room, including the composers Boyce and Hart—that this promising (maybe even great) song could use a good hook at its start. So Shelton pulled apart the song's primary G chord and developed an earworm hook on the spot. He plucked the G and its octave on the first two beats, descending to the F, E, and D suspended over two beats, and three descending notes on each beat. A hook. A catchy hook to lead off the song. Primed for Top 40 radio. Shelton received no public acknowledgment for this contribution. No shared songwriting credit. No royalties. He took his AFM rates and split. Credit came with the next job and the next and the next. And credit developed through a reputation sustaining a life-long career as musician and producer.

Shelton rewarded the Monkees project with his sharp contributions, both the standout hook and his guitar craftsmanship in general. In turn, the system rewarded him with remuneration and reputation. Credit came through the world of LA: the gossip of studio musicians, recording engineers, and the ecosystem of exchange in the tight world of its recording studios.

Shelton's twangy guitar hook jumpstarting "Clarksville" actuated the calculus underscoring the various elements of the system. His on-the-spot addition of this hook betrays how far, wide, and deep the values of this artworld, this system, permeated its various parts and participants. The Top 40 clock that diagrammed radio programming for DJs did not loom over Shelton in the studio. He absorbed the needs of the system and brought it to a focus in this hook. From Boyce and Hart's composition to the recording studio and engineers to the role of Top 40 radio programming, the nexus of different elements of the system, most networked in Los Angeles itself, came together to produce this shimmering rock classic.

2
"Ben Frank's-Types"

The address: 8585 Sunset Boulevard, Hollywood, California. The place: Ben Frank's coffee shop, a major hangout for youth and a major brewing place for the Monkees.

When Bob Rafelson and Bert Schneider, two young television producers, dialed in on the global sensation of the Beatles, seeking to channel the countercultural camaraderie, subversive humor and pop music energy of the Fab Four's films *A Hard Day's Night* (1964) and *Help!* (1965) into a TV series—soon named *The Monkees*—they felt confident tuning into the Sunset Strip, and this coffee shop, to find their foursome. The Strip's signification radiated on the same spectrum, a global to local bandwidth: long hair, skinny lapels, tight cuffs around their ankles, snazzy boots, and sardonic smirks, all found floating through the British Invasion and the 8000 blocks of Sunset Boulevard. The producers pinpointed this particular place, Ben Frank's, as a Beatlesque barometer: they wanted Beatlesque boys, mod clothes, and Bohemian vibes. So the upstart producers placed a highly coded audition ad for aspiring talent in the central Los Angeles trade papers *Daily Variety* and the *Hollywood Reporter* on September 8, 1965.

"Spirited Ben Frank's-types," the ad broadcasted cheerily, in a code only decipherable by someone in Los Angeles familiar with its cultural, sociopolitical, and industrial landscape and signs. The ad represents a sign about signs, seeking new signs and sign-ups.

Full of signification. Moreover, the ad's reference to "Ben Frank's" reveals how strongly a national, even international, mass media industrial project like the Monkees—a TV show synched with the release of recorded music products, tapping into the global phenomenon of the Beatles and the British Invasion—retained highly localized roots: in this case, the Sunset Strip and its "Ben Frank's-types," along with the industrial media complex intersecting its Hollywood landscape.

Ben Frank's coffee shop was a masterpiece of jet-age architecture, with its flying triangular ceiling and cavernous sense of space, an exemplary model of "Googie" style, the futurist aesthetic blasting off in mid-century southern California. The 24-hour diner's interior soared with dynamic, modern vigor, a commercial vernacular spirit, welding modernist elements of abstraction and progressivism with popular design. Its exposed architectural beams sliced through the restaurant's atmosphere in strong lines that suggested a special effects show, a bit over the top but also sleek and unpretentious at the same time. If these beams remained, as one critic described this

MADNESS!!
AUDITIONS
Folk & Roll Musicians-Singers
for **acting roles in new TV series.**
Running parts for 4 insane boys, age 17-21.
Want spirited Ben Frank's-types.
Have courage to work.
Must come down for interview.
CALL: HO. 6-5188

Finding the global in the local: a coded ad targeting a Hollywood hangout as a source for the fabricated Beatlesque band.

style, "unhindered by accepted taste,"[1] they also seemed unhindered by gravity, though they functioned as authentic load-bearing tubular-steel supports; their flagrant exposure in the mise-en-scène of the restaurant highlighted the sense of adventure injected into the ambiance here, turning an A-frame support beam into Hollywood set design as it collapsed deep into the diner's frame and then jutted up again, lending it an energetic slant in the front and the rear.[2]

The high ceilings of Ben Frank's invited people in, offering a sense of reception, openness, and expansiveness: come in and hang out. There is space here. Room to roam and relax, let go, connect, see and be seen—the opposite of old-fashioned, low-ceilinged, dark restaurants, which enforced intimacy in closed-off booths, cloaked encounters in dim light.

Ben Frank's became a hangout almost immediately after its launch as a stirring satellite on the Strip in 1962, a conjunction of the emerging youth subcultures and an architecture that embraced the modern spirit. "Googie accustoms the people to expect strangeness," an early observer noted, "and makes them the readier for those strange things yet to come which will truly make good sense."[3] A prophetic remark, as Ben Frank's found young customers ready to stir up strange things that made good sense, like rock and roll, more progressive lifestyles, and youth-driven protests.

The emphasis on space and the modern extended out into the coffee shop's surrounding landscape: namely, its parking lot, which ran along the building's entire eastern facade, with windows stretching from the wall facing the lot to that fronting the street. The panoramic panes of glass acknowledged the location as a destination for the car, embracing its modernity and mobility, and especially the freedom they lent to youth. This transparency confirmed that boulevards and rapid transportation represented the "now." In other words, Ben Frank's didn't hide the outside world of cars from its patrons; the parking lot belonged to the scenery and space. The diner's Cinemascope-sized windows splashed the

The counterculture congregates at Ben Frank's.

exterior into the interior, inviting the cars zipping down the Sunset Strip and into the diner's parking lot, with all their energetic, shiny colors and lights, into the restaurant: a movie screen of mobility. And the parking lot itself organically tied into the rendezvous space of the overall scene as it too offered a hangout, a place for meeting up before entering the establishment or afterwards, continuing the conversation as you hovered around the cars. It too was a space, a public sphere, acknowledged in the design of the building. Indeed, according to legend and lore, two major 1960s Los Angeles bands formed in the parking lot of Ben Frank's: Buffalo Springfield and Love. Strange things. Good sense.

This emphasis on the modern and the progressive, community, and cars all aligned with and invited in a youth subculture, turning Ben Frank's into a major destination for teenagers newly mobile with cars and migrating to the Strip for its rock and roll.

What is a "Ben Frank's-type?" It is the kind of kid that frugged at the clubs up and down the Sunset Strip before or after decamping at the 24-hour coffee shop. Ben Frank's-types took over the nightlife and culture of the Sunset Strip at this time, rapidly replacing the old Hollywood ersatz-ritz red vinyl booth scene—dry martinis and sweat-beaded champagne buckets—on this unincorporated stretch of 1.7 miles of road. Ben Frank's-types hung out at the coffee shop just for the vibe, for the pooled connections, to be seen on the scene, and to see others on the scene. They patronized new rock clubs like the Whisky a Go Go, four blocks down, on 8901 Sunset Boulevard, which opened in 1964—only a little over a year before the Monkees ad got placed—to a sensational seismic signification across the 1960s semiotic stratosphere, with magazine, television, and long-playing coverage. There you'd find Ben Frank's-types dancing under the spell of the sounds spun by DJ Patty Brockhurst in her shimmering skirt and her cage above the crowded dance floor. Yes, a cage, suspended above the club's interior to save space, but a decision that ultimately generated a whole new symbolism, for once she started spontaneously and sincerely shimmying to the records she spun, she transformed from a spinner of sonic sensations into a sexualized symbol, as spellbinding as the sounds of music spurring the whole scene. "Go-Go" skirted through her moves and her signs.

Ben Frank's-types caught these vibes, and they spread up and down the Strip. The Whisky owners picked up on these sizzling signs and quickly installed more cages and hired two more girls to simply shake and swerve to the sounds, mirroring the moves on the floor below. One of the new caged birds designed her own outfit—a dress with a bare midriff and fringe—and it soon became the media symbol for a new phenomenon: the go-go girl, shaking everywhere through popular culture.[4]

Ben Frank's-types and go-go girls, then, sprang from the same fertile 1960s Los Angeles milieu and quickly migrated to the mainstream. Go-go girls popped up on TV everywhere, from *The Monkees*—alongside its leading Ben Frank's-types—to *Laugh-In*. Even Batman, the hipless wonder, shimmied like a go-go girl on his TV show, doing "The Batusi."

Time magazine covered the Whisky a Go Go and the surrounding Sunset Strip scene within months. That same year the BBC sent Top of the Pops host Jimmy Savile to report on the club. Record labels jumped on the buzz by quickly cutting a "live" album (heavily re-recorded) from the club, *Johnny Rivers at the Whisky à Go Go*, which popularized the venue almost as much as the singer.[5] The liner notes described the scene as one for "adolescents who want to be adults and adults who want to be adolescents."

The Whisky got go-going because Ben Frank's-types transformed the Sunset Strip, the boulevard hosting all these clubs, into a teenager hub, a center for rock and roll nightlife. Another hip club, The Trip, opened just across the street from Ben Frank's at 8572 Sunset. The Sea Witch, at 8514 Sunset, represented "one of the teenie-bopper IN SPOTS," according to local avant-garde rocker Frank Zappa, who included a map with descriptions of the "Hot Spots" on the Strip in the gatefold cover of the first issues of his band's 1966 album *Freak Out!* A few blocks over, at 8433 Sunset, you could find Ciro's Le Disc, a rebranded club to compete with the Whisky, later renamed It's Boss, a "teenie-bopper heaven" by Zappa's call. Two blocks down from that you'd run into The Fifth Estate, itself a block from a central meeting spot for "Striplings" (another nickname for the teens clogging the sidewalks), Pandora's Box at 8118 Sunset.[6]

Ben Frank's-types, then, elevated Sunset into the rival, if not the replacement, of "Swinging London." No surprise, in turn, that this cultural center populated with Ben Frank's-types drew in the Rolling Stones, Them, the Beatles, the Yardbirds, and other great British Invasion bands. "This cross-continental camaraderie occurred," as one scenester affirmed, "just as each city was experiencing its musical and artistic zenith."[7] Ben Frank's-types, in this sense, held tangible meanings and associations in this geographic and historical moment. They signified the rise of a youth movement, the Sunset Strip youth culture—the counterculture, if you will. This youth culture embraced and flaunted values for their oppositional meaning to the adult world: the owners, the realtors, the police. Those values remained fraught with a festering sense of resistance that would seem almost inevitable when activated by confrontational events in 1966 and early 1967.

These conflicts took off in response to crackdowns by the police on the swarms of youth cruising the Strip's sidewalks, seen as a blight by real estate owners and planners. Investors and landlords pressured politicians, who, in turn, coerced the cops to get control over the youth scene—Ben Frank's-types—if not outright eliminate it. In this regard, Ben Frank's-types ran through the "riot on the Strip" in 1966 when local politicians and the police dredged up an old unenforced curfew law and began busting kids for cruising past the 10 p.m. deadline, with arrests hitting the thousands in the summer of 1966.[8] "Vagrancy—that's what everybody got busted for," recalled Gail Zappa of those days.[9] Meanwhile, establishment rag the *Los Angeles Times* pushed stories of teens and crime on the Strip with admittedly witty headlines like "Hard Day's Night on the Strip." Still, most of the press understood these tensions as symptoms of the old establishment smarting from the downturn of their businesses and culture in the area, and its transformation into a rock and youth scene.

Youth and their sympathizers—many leading figures in the local music industry—challenged the authorities by forming a committee to fight back in the press, with printed fliers and radio DJs helping to promote rallies and gatherings drawing attention to their plight, fighting for their right to assemble peacefully and meaningfully, to find a culture and camaraderie in a space they were making their own. This resistance tied their youthful protests to larger movements across the country, a symbolic resonance recognized even by the local power's opposition, who cited, as justification for their strained Strip surveillance and crackdowns, the recent state "anti-riot" legislation passed in response to the Watts riots and Berkeley's free-speech movement.[10]

These conflicts exploded in November 1966 when thousands of youths gathered at an organized protest in front of Pandora's Box, with stars like Peter Fonda and Sonny and Cher speaking and performing on their behalf. The crowds spilled out onto the streets, blocking traffic, with many of the teens jumping on the roofs of stalled buses, waving their signs well after curfew. Deputies cracked down on the protestors, violently attacking some and arresting hundreds. Such harsh confrontations inspired more protests over the subsequent weekends and almost regularly into 1967. In that year, Buffalo Springfield (recall their formation in the parking lot of Ben Frank's) released "For What It's Worth," a song inspired by the protests but one that would take on a much broader meaning for the country's youth counterculture, demonstrating how this local phenomenon circuited with national and even global significance.

Ben Frank's-types one and all, and all for one.

These Sunset Strip conflicts represent a time jump from the original Monkees audition ad in 1965. However, the "Ben Frank's-types" selected for the TV show eventually honored their connection—and sympathy—to the protestors, and the recent local conflicts, on an episode of *The Monkees* show in January 1967; in a post-episode interview, in which the individual members speak off the cuff as themselves, the Monkees expressed their sympathy for the youth in revolt. The group defended the rights of the protestors, pushing back on the characterization of their actions as "riots" and insisting on calling them "demonstrations."[11]

Yet a "Ben Frank's-type" also signaled an exclusionary tactic in the original Monkees audition ad. It meant—along with the "folk and roll" designation—that the producers wanted white boys, tacitly omitting anyone from the many ethnic and racialized musical subcultures enriching different parts of Los Angeles. The designation distinguished the applicants from any Mexican or Black subcultural types, ones digging the city's sounds of Mexican-laced pop, soul, or rhythm and blues. A "Ben Frank's-type," then, separated the aspirants from anyone coming out of the R&B scene around Central Avenue.

A Ben Frank's-type would also include artists and patrons of the Los Angeles art scene, which sprouted up in the 1950s and early 1960s and spiraled through the same signifying scenery, from the Sunset Strip to West Hollywood and North Beverly Hills, just below the Strip. Artists and their supporters populated the same hangouts, from Ben Frank's to Ciro's to the Whisky and Barney's Beanery (immortalized in the Pop artist Ed Kienholz's 1965 life-size statuary piece, *The Beanery*).

London and New York launched Pop art, but Los Angeles embraced it, enhanced it, and played a crucial role in its blast-off. Anyway, Los Angeles proved perfect for Pop, already Pop, and always already Pop.[12]

Indeed, Los Angeles gave Andy Warhol one of his big breaks, his first major exhibit, and a bigger splash as a Pop artist with a 1962 show, his rows of Campbell's Soup Cans, at the Ferus Gallery on 723 North La Cienega Boulevard, a 15-minute walk from Ben Frank's, just under a mile. Everett Ellin's nearby gallery (on Sunset) featured shows by Pop artists like Claes Oldenburg's zany, fast-food "soft sculptures": oversized ice cream cones; humongous Good Humor bars in cartoony flavors like orange leopard and green tiger.

The Pop artists embraced the fleeting yet vital spirit of popular culture and the playful insolence of recognizing popular culture alongside the values and traditions of the fine arts. The novelty of Los Angeles—its campy architecture, car culture, Hollywood glitz, and relative newness—embodied the Pop art spirit. The first Pop art exhibition in the United States happened at the Pasadena Art Museum in 1962, titled "New Painting of Common Objects," with numerous West Coast Pop artists represented in the show. Displaying alongside iconic works by Andy Warhol and Roy Lichtenstein of comic books, celebrities, and commodities blown up to the size of traditional fine art paintings, West Coast artist Ed Ruscha presented his glossy reproductions of gas stations, canned food graphic design, and advertising billboards; Wayne Thiebaud's gooey tactile paintings of pudding and pastry counter displays or pinball machines; Jim Dine's and Joe Goode's sculptural paintings combining fine art frames and everyday consumer objects.

A *Los Angeles Times* cartoon mocking the early Warhol show featured two Ben Frank's-types—at the very least, two barefoot beatniks—declaring the "Zen feeling" they got from chicken noodle soup. The cartoon echoed the outré art critic Max Kozloff's lament that Pop art, with its celebration of our commodified popular culture, corrupted his sacral galleries with a "pinheaded and contemptible style of gum chewers, [and] bobby soxers," an anachronistic description of adolescents (or Ben Frank's-types).[13] Kozloff and the cartoonist shared complaints about Pop art infecting the fine arts, virally spreading from the new consumer youth market and its mass media, primarily comic books and rock. Pop art blurred the boundaries between hallowed fine art traditions and consumer culture, outraging critics and earnest observers, who balked at such effrontery, and framed much of their ire over Pop art through the lens of its new audiences and the artists themselves as youthful delinquents, pimply patrons and practitioners of the new power of pop.

News stories on Pop art, even most sympathetic or enthusiastic ones, collapsed the movement with youthful pop culture, music, films, and fashion, frequently equating Warhol with the latest go-go dance moves. When *Time* magazine devoted an issue to "Today's Teen-Agers" in January 1965, they commissioned Warhol for his signature silk screen cover artwork. As a critic argued in an early defense of Pop art, the teen associations of the movement resonated with its opposition to tradition and standard values.[14]

In Los Angeles, the worlds of pop and Pop art mingled. Michelle Phillips, the languorous singer from the Mamas and Papas, made regular visits to the Ferus Gallery, as did Toni Basil when she took time off from dancing behind Sonny and Cher, while the Pop artist

Billy Al Bengston caught the Byrds at Ciro's; LA Pop artist Ed Ruscha danced at the Whisky and Ciro's; artist Larry Bell worked at the Unicorn coffeehouse on Sunset (just down the street from Barney's Beanery), where the Kingston Trio played, and where David Crosby met Jim Dickson, who would merge and manage him with some other musicians to form the Byrds. "It's Boss" splashed its club walls with posters in the style of Roy Lichtenstein's comic book prints of Dick Tracy and Little Orphan Annie, and its exterior sign buzzed with mod-Pop art ambience in its word balloon bubble-shaped neon.[15]

In 1963, Warhol returned to the Ferus with a 7-foot Elvis in the window of the gallery and silk screen prints of Elizabeth Taylor linking Pop art to Hollywood and vice versa. Traveling to LA for this second major show, Warhol recounted years later—in prose pitched perfectly by his ghostwriter—that the more they moved west, the more "Pop" things got: billboards, diner design, junk food stands, kooky architecture, and movie ads all employed amusement-park-style flourishes and performative decor and embellishments. That same year the Ferus Gallery hosted a show by Warhol's Pop art compatriot Roy Lichtenstein, with the show's poster featuring a tube sock in his distinctive comic book graphics. When Warhol returned to New York, he dubbed his studio "The Factory," an insolent homage to Hollywood's alleged assembly-line mode of production of mass media generally denigrated by New York's fine art elite. In Los Angeles, few would bat an eye at the gesture.

Driving home the connection between Pop art and the Sunset Strip pop-rock scene, Ed Ruscha conceived an art project that tied together the changes transforming the culture not only here in LA, but the world over: the way neighborhoods depended on and catered to car culture, to the youth, and his fascination as an outsider (along with that of the rest of us) with LA. In homage to the mobility of a modern youth culture centered so much on clubs, cruising and hangouts like Ben Frank's, Ruscha created a serial photographic pamphlet that unfolded like an accordion with head-on snapshots of every building on the Sunset Strip.

When Warhol toured Los Angeles, he took the necessary trip to the Sunset Strip and Ben Frank's, the whole scene passing the fifteen-minute audition for the great Pop artist. All that signification seeded in the original "Ben Frank's-types" ad. Signs and wonder. Signs and space. All the signs on the Sunset Strip.

The ad itself signified an interpretation, a take on authentic Ben Frank's-types (whatever authentic means in a space full of signs). The ad's posting in the trade magazines indicated the selection of a preselected type: aspirants already committed to the industry, its processes, and its system. In other words, the ad also signaled an industry endeavor. Anyone responding to the ad, the ad itself assumed, as did its placement in a business bible, already proved their commitment to the industry's logic (indeed, the four finalists all retained connections previously established in the business). And the ad assumed most or all the aspirants had already arrived in LA, an adventurous journey itself signaling an alignment with the processes of the pop industry as well as an understanding of the local culture and what it signified—"Ben Frank's-type"—both for the region and the mass media industry backing up the ad.

As a sign, Ben Frank's-types sustained their signifying power through the semiotic soiree of the Sunset Strip. Yet they surged with a symbolism suspended in mass media: the Beatles' hair, flippant attitude, and playfulness. In this latter regard, the ad understood and signaled that knowledge to its applicants, that Ben Frank's-types represented a local variation on a national or international type: beatniks, hipsters, long hairs—basically, Beatles-types. That Beatle signification stimulated the whole project. No surprise, then, that such figures as Danny Hutton (later with Three Dog Night), Keith Allison (later with Paul Revere and the Raiders), Stephen Stills, and Paul Williams all recall auditioning for the parts. According to production memos, the producers passed on the rising eclectic

Warhol surveys the Sunset Strip, and its signs (Ben Frank's directly behind).

pop musician Van Dyke Parks (submitted by his agent), who soon collaborated with Brian Wilson, before signing with Warner Bros. Records as a solo artist. Most of the applicants scored reports of "too straight," "too sophisticated," or "too extreme" according to screen test memos.[16]

The selection process weighed the impact of the different Monkees on the potential TV market numbers. "To succeed on network television," one of the executives explained later, "you had to attract at least thirty percent of the audience. The thought was that our group had to be demographically diverse."[17] The final four summed up this calculation: a Brit to capture the British Invasion, two bashful clowns, and a Texan with some country-and-western flair.

The show's pilot script—dated August 17, almost a month before the audition ad—reveals that the young British performer Davy Jones had already scored a key part in the project as it introduces "DAVY FORBES" as one of the "Monkeys," describing the character as "small" and "adorable," a fitting portrait of the real Davy, nineteen years old at the time, tiny (a former jockey), and indeed a cuddly toy as cute as a Beatle.[18] A child star in London on stage, radio, and television, Jones earned a Tony nomination as the Artful Dodger in *Oliver!* when the West End production ran on Broadway in 1963. That nabbed him a talent contract from Columbia Pictures/Screen Gems Television, which started placing him in bit roles on TV shows, as well as a campaign to turn him into a pop singer. Colpix—the record division of Columbia Pictures—released his first single and artlessly slapped together a self-titled album in 1965 with sappy, generic arrangements of pop songs that quickly vanished in the air and on the charts. But with Columbia's Screen Gems backing *The Monkees* TV show, they slotted Jones immediately into the project. He even helped with the casting crawl, canvassing the Sunset Strip club scene with one of the TV executives as they took in performances by Sonny and Cher, the Modern Folk Quartet, and Love.

After flunking out of college by choice, Peter Tork toted his guitar and five-string banjo (he could play piano, ukulele, and the French horn, according to early Monkees promotional material) to New York's Greenwich Village, where he blew through amateur nights at hide-away cafes ("pass the hat" through the crowd for any compensation) and small folk clubs, soaking up the scene, eventually hitching on a small tour with the Phoenix Singers as an accompanist. With little success in bohemia, Tork moved to Long Beach—a short freeway stretch from Los Angeles—in 1965, playing piano at the Golden Bear in Huntington Beach with the Buffalo Fish, alongside Ron Lang and Stephen Stills (future Buffalo Springfield members). Stills told Tork about "a TV show based on A Hard Day's Night" and the audition ad and encouraged him to try out. (Indeed, of the final Monkees, only Tork answered the original ad; the others auditioned through their agents or business connections.) Tork's audition reel starts with him pronouncing the entire alphabet—consonants and vowels—like a word unto itself, a bit of Carrollian nonsense that John Lennon would likely appreciate. He probably landed the job right then and there, but he brought his guitar, riffed a bit on it but riffed more on his humor, and even shamelessly drew attention to his Beatles haircut with a joke. Sold.

A native Texan, Michael Nesmith carried his drawl, guitar, and ambition to Los Angeles and immediately hit the club circuit, winding his way through Ledbetter's and the Troubadour, proving himself a stage presence and a good country-and-western singer with a touch of the early 1960s folk sound. He put on solo acts, joined a group or two, and often acted as hootmaster for the Troubadour's Monday night hootenannies, a job he held for almost two years. Nesmith had only learned guitar a few years earlier, at age nineteen, yet taught himself enough to write several songs published by Randy Sparks and, starting in 1963, released three singles on small labels. The Monkees' producers called the Troubadour's owner as part of their survey for talent and he recommended Nesmith, whom they came to see perform. His audition reel unspools with confidence, snark, and wit, all leavened with his easy twang.

The son of a working character actor, Micky Dolenz grew up in the industry, starring as a child in the TV series *Circus Boy* for its two seasons (1956–7). After finishing high school, Dolenz jumped back into the biz, picking up an agent and appearances on TV shows like *Peyton Place*; he joined a band, a few actually, as a singer and guitarist, with one, the Missing Links, even releasing a go-nowhere single (a link the whole world missed). At the time of his Monkee tryout, Dolenz, in the heat of pilot season, ran through auditions for three or four other programs that month, coincidentally all shows trying to tap into the pop music scene. His audition reel captures the comedy in his music making and the music—all rhythm, timing, and pitch—in his comic banter.

Thus began a band formulated in the laboratory of the media industry, blending the television and music businesses, using songwriters and musicians to produce the music, while the "band" acted it out and mimed the music on the TV show—all coordinated by a central command center. Even the band's name sprang from the management team, who explained its logic as a reference to the current trend indebted to the Beatles, à la the Byrds (who misspelled their name for the same reason). While some initial discussion took place about hiring an actual band to front the TV show or letting the hired crew perform their own music, the emphasis given to the performances on the TV show overruled these prospects, enforcing the game plan of using professional songwriters and session musicians to handle the music (and the auditions indicated that acting played a more critical role in the casting).

By the mid-1960s, rock culture upended the pop music business as the performers now acted as their own songwriters, with the Beatles and Bob Dylan standing out as the new role models: one of the many ways they both revolutionized music. Audiences and critics, in turn, now expected artists to write and perform their

Adding up the equation to the final prefab four.

own music. From the auditions to the songwriting, musical accompaniment, and recording, the Monkees project operated through a process eclipsed by its very inspiration, the Beatles. Pop art irony masked the old-fashioned entertainment business logic behind the whole enterprise.

The charade of the Monkees lingered under the surface of almost every early article on the band. The otherwise enthusiastic fan-based cheer of *KRLA Beat*, a local radio-sponsored fanzine, withered with skepticism at the leading public relations pushed on them about the band, noting their amateur status on their instruments and the recording process in general. Another article referred to them as "assembly line products." It framed the Monkees as fruit from the robust "family tree" of RCA Victor and Colgems, moving on to document the abundant commercial returns of the Monkees to their corporate creators. This article noted the success of their first single and album, already clocking up a million sales. "The ironic part of the Monkees' disc success is that the studio musicians," the article revealed, "not the Monkees themselves, were used on both 'Last Train to Clarksville' and their album." Even early articles, like one built around a discussion with the behind-the-scenes team of the Monkees' producers and songwriters Bobby Hart and Tommy Boyce on writing and producing the band, made transparent the machinery behind the product, exposing the studio musicians that backed up the performers, the process of dealing with talent selected from an audition, and the guidance of management. As Davy Jones explained to *Newsweek* in a 1966 article: "This isn't a rock 'n' roll group. It's an act."[19]

All the early publicity highlighted the auditions—skipping out on the already contracted or connected candidates—and frequently quoted the "Ben Frank's-types" ad. To top it all off, the production company's promotional material for the show flagrantly flaunted the amateur status of the Monkees: "Like their prototypes the Beatles: 'They have musical inclinations and have been known to play in tune (though admittedly not always playing the same tune at the same time).'" Another widely placed advertisement—running everywhere from TV *Guide* to the industry trade magazines—read: "Are they real? Are they believable? Are they kidding?" That spirit informed most of the upcoming *Monkees* TV series advertising as they all relished in the cheeky, "Put-On" spirit of the times, with Pop art word balloons declaring, "There's No Business like Monkee Business." One ad doubled down on the heart of the enterprise, asking rhetorically and insolently: "Who's putting who on?"

Indeed, the sham occasionally completely broke through in headlines like "Formula for Pop Success" and "Mad Man-Made Monkees." Flip inside the issue with the last headline, and the accompanying article spelled it out on the title page: "TV ASSEMBLY LINE THAT BUILT BEATLE-TYPE MONKEES." The writer began with the story of the *Daily Variety* ad, its producers, and the auditions under the lead: "American know-how can produce anything—even a manufactured imitation of the Beatles." Then came a surprise, according to the author: "Studio musicians taped the music for the records. The Monkees? They sang."[20] Notably, the article sprang from a TV news magazine in Detroit, a town with the know-how of factory-machine manufacturing.

To take another example, *Love Letters to the Monkees*, a 1967 paperback sponsored by their producers, featured a letter confessing:

> My girlfriend Irma says she found out that you really don't sing your songs, and other people sing for you.
>
> I don't believe you don't sing your songs.
>
> I love all your songs, but maybe you don't sing them so then I like not your music but whoever sings for you. But I really like you. Good-bye.
>
> Melissa B.
> Cincinnati, Ohio

And the book left the letter unanswered. Melissa and Irma would have to figure it out on their own. All this shows that the producers anticipated the question of authenticity in formulating the Monkees project and rigged the issue in their favor, folding it into the cheeky, ironic, and Pop attitude characterizing their promotion. They dressed up their experiment in manufacturing a band from inside the Hollywood factory in Pop's "Put-On" philosophy. It fit like a Mickey Mouse glove.

From the start, then, the Monkees project—and the Monkees themselves—floated a gleefully carefree attitude about the whole act, almost flaunting the artifice and commerce of the pop music industry (an attitude itself picked up or ripped off from the Beatles). Everything about the Monkees accentuated the fabrication of the industry. Like Andy Warhol's Factory—a concept that mocked the Romantic myth of individual artistic genius as outdated even while it modernized it to the age of celebrity—the Monkees foregrounded the industry of their medium with a cheery and almost reckless

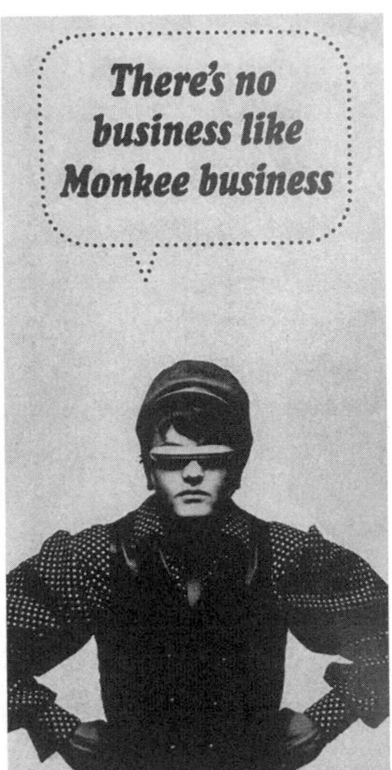

Monkees promotion evoking Pop art.

abandon. Every early article on the group narrated the casting call that generated the band, the producers behind the show, the audience research, the packaging by music and TV producers, and facts like the challenging industrial schedule surrounding the Monkees.

The problem of the Monkees for rock purists wasn't just their camp attitude of anti-seriousness, not only or merely their Pop art dethroning of seriousness, for rock had yet to scale a highbrow dimension of respectability and stature. The Monkees project also suggested a kind of insider-hipster conceptualism. It seemed almost like an experiment: what if someone could bring together songsmiths, studio musicians, producers, screenwriters, and an entire assemblage of media specialists, synchronize their craft and talent, and sell it in the marketplace? Poof! A band out of thin air!

No origins or struggles. A machine-made band. From this angle, the Monkees retained a conceptual aura like Marcel Duchamp's Readymades or Warhol's Factory exercises that reverberated with the pop Dadaism of the TV show, with its sped-up frame rates, jerky jump cuts, slapstick-cartoon energy, and absurdist narrative logic.

Tapping into a camp and "Put-On" attitude tuned the Monkees in with the hippest channels on the mid-1960s cultural airwaves. The Monkees came at the cusp of a period of incredible cross-fertilization in the arts and mass media as Pop art networked with television, film, and graphic design and vice versa. Pop art raided the world of popular media and consumerism, translating them into subjects for paintings and sculptures: a giant tube of toothpaste, comic book frames, cartoon characters. In doing so, the Pop artists collapsed traditions that clearly distinguished between high and low art, turning comic book images, the sharp, glossy graphic design of consumer products, and advertising into bold, striking paintings. In a potent fusion, strains of popular media quickly absorbed Pop art's perspective on itself. This self-conscious turn in popular media eradicated any of the potentially patronizing perspectives of Pop art and added an ironic spin, a celebratory one, to it. Popular media assimilated the tone and tropes of Pop art, injecting the former with the revitalized energy unleashed by the latter. Album covers, advertisements, and movies infused Pop art vivacity into their work, as did *The Monkees* TV show. *TV Guide* commissioned Warhol himself to design a cover, a four-panel profile of hit series *Get Smart*'s Agent 99 awash in primary colors. The instant camp classic Boob Tube show *Batman* featured a Pop art title sequence and sound balloons in thick lines and primary colors: "Bam!" "Splatt!" "Kapow!"

Scanning this scene, the overnight intellectual celebrity Susan Sontag dubbed it a "new sensibility," in which distinctions between high and low culture collapsed through a rich appreciation of popular media, expanding beyond the privileged realm of the fine arts. In this new culture, by Sontag's measure, audiences could value classic works of high modernism while also admitting to the beauty of machinery, cars, and a song by the Supremes or the Beatles. From her perspective, the widely known fact that the new painters dug "the new sound" of rock and pop signaled not simply a casual lifestyle tic but a more expansive form of thinking. Sontag's essay resonated with her more notorious analysis of "camp," the cultural sensibility that relished kitsch and artifice and exaggeration in the arts, from over-the-top melodramas to bad science-fiction films to cheesy songs. In the essay, Sontag recognized the relationship between camp and Pop art and even characterized rock as a "camp" art form, glossing on its French term "yé-yé." Rock was often a "Put-On," a kind of campy romp, from Little Richard to Jerry Lee Lewis to novelty songs that repeatedly magnified the comic undertones of the medium. Elsewhere, Sontag honed her analysis down to a precise equation: "Pop art is Beatles art," practically a formula for the Monkees.[21]

The New Journalist Tom Wolfe agreed with Sontag's axiom, characterizing rock as a "sort of Pop art" in his essays on radio disc jockeys, new dance crazes, and the "teen tycoon" Phil Spector. In surveying this "Pop Society," Wolfe's sociology itself turned his subjects and language into a vehicle of pop expression, zinging adjectives, hammering and tapping out punctuation like a rhythm section, an impressionistic whirl, like a New Wave swish-pan of streaking neon, calling the "New Culture Makers" grown-ups in teen fashion styles.[22]

Wolfe's journalistic colleagues Robert Benton and David Newman celebrated this new sensibility, or "new sentimentality," by creating an original survey of its values. An exegetical sermon, their piece shares with Sontag's "On Camp" both the year of publication (1964) and a kind of new dandyism, flippancy, attention to surface and style: clothes, looks, attitude, whatever is hip, fresh, au courant, insolently flaunting this elevation of appearances. Published in *Esquire*, then a slick outlet for the New Journalism, Benton and Newman elevated specific icons of the new sensibility and tossed aside arbiters of the old. The piece itself retains a sense of irony (a key value). It discards anything that smacks of overt earnestness (from Arthur Miller to Jackson Pollock to Elvis). While rooted in an insider-hipster coolness and proffering a set of new icons and values, the writing suggests a sense of a rather hasty and all too willing readiness to dismiss and abandon beliefs. But that speed signifies part of the new value system, recognizing the pace and energy of modern life. Even if the authors remain genuinely passionate about nouvelle vague film directors like Jean-Luc Godard and François Truffaut or the sartorial style of Jackie Kennedy, they sense the joke of their pop pantheism. How exhilarating to think of these contemporary cultural icons as gods of a new set of values! Of course, the Beatles made the cut, cast in self-conscious commercialism and Warholian irony: "The Beatles. They are the Put-On; the big laugh; Professionalism; the new idea of the Celebrity." Likewise, in their eyes, Leo Castelli, the gallery owner and primary dealer of Pop art, stood heroically for "money made in mockery." And rock and roll was flagrantly and unapologetically "calculated, cynical." As Benton and Newman held out:

> In the New, your primary objective is to make your life fit your style. There is Professionalism above all. For example, the Old concept "selling out," which used to drive good men crazy, causing them to cry in their beer and bemoan their wasted talent (writing ad copy, for instance) has disappeared. Now we glory in what pros we are, and a man loves himself for writing the best jingle on the market.[23]

Bam! Splatt! Kapow!

Money made from mockery. Professionalism. Calculation. Selling out. Conscious commercialism. Jingles. The Put-On. All these elements couldn't jive more strongly with the Monkees project. From the perspective of camp and the new sensibility, to find the Monkees overly commercial or sell-outs represented an expired attitude, a sign of earnest squareness. Of course, they're a sell-out—that's part of the joke, part of the new sensibility. It's a great Put-On. Get with it.

Like the Pop artists, the creators of the Monkees (including the Monkees themselves) found vitality in the practice of appropriation, locating something vibrant in our modern culture and tapping into its energy to create the new, thereby promoting and expanding its spirit. Appropriation mocked the myth of authenticity (a value itself only a human construct, after all). It recognized the mechanism of repetition in the commercial cycle of modern media industries; Pop art, then, licensed media practitioners to self-consciously spin this cycle as part of the artwork. By taking the Beatles as their inspiration or template, the producers of the Monkees recognized, of course, the commercial value of the Fab Four. But they also appreciated their difference from red-vinyl cocktail crooners like Lawrence Welk, Frank Sinatra, or Dean Martin, from the old sentimentality. Appropriation identifies conventions possibly replicable for repeated success. But it can also signify—as with the Monkees project—genuine resonance, sympathy, and inspiration. Strange things and good sense.

3
The Genius of the System

The address 7033 Sunset Boulevard, which housed the offices of the Screen Gems-Columbia Music song publishing company, commanded the most important base of operations for the Monkees project. The whole multimedia endeavor originated with Raybert, a television company contracted with Columbia Studios and the movie company's television wing. Yet the TV show depended on the music division to sustain the concept at its core: the depiction of the Monkees as a band. The show required music and musical performances to string together the whole operation. To bring the Beatles model to life, like the films that inspired the show, the songs were crucial to the audience's investment in the program's premise. In this way, the music arguably propped up the entire Monkees enterprise, more than the TV show. Indeed, when "Last Train to Clarksville" hit the top spot followed by the first album, and then the chartbusting "I'm a Believer," the music soon outperformed the show in numbers and revenue. These offices, then, were the headquarters for Monkeemania.

Screen Gems' address, in fact, reveals one of the key advantages of working in a hub, near other collaborators but also close to competitors, particularly in a creative industry like music. Housing your biz in an area crawling with aspiring "employees" (songwriters or performers), going door to door for work, saves on the expenses of recruitment or scouting: what one sociologist calls "spatially dependent transactions cost."[1] Spatially dependent transactions: in other words, schlepping all over the country to scout for new talent.

Screen Gems and all its neighboring Hollywood music companies gain from their proximity to the gravitational pull of songwriters and save on the "spatially dependent costs" in searching out a Tommy Boyce, Bobby Hart, or Michael Nesmith. Instead, the cost of such activity—traveling—falls on the aspirant. Boyce, Hart, Nesmith, and others like them cover that cost—a self-directed investment in their own talent—when they sell their songs (or eat the costs if they fail). The trip to Los Angeles, pounding the pavement to pursue publishers, counts as the songwriter's investment in their own enterprise. The proximity of the different, competing publishers risks losing a Boyce to a competitor, but the gains—in cost-cutting (the labor market search, scouting for songwriters) and in information—outweigh this risk. For example, if a publisher hears a Boyce and Hart song, rejects it, and then sees it turn into a hit for a competitor, the losing publisher still gains a little knowledge of the next trend, and thereby informs their writers to cook up something similar ("folk and roll" after the success of the Byrds or surf-rock after the Beach Boys).

Think, in this regard, of the high turnover of failed artists and, more significantly, the ever-changing number of musicians and songwriters moving to the city, some breaking and some bailing after failure. Think, moreover, of the ancillary markets of nightclubs essentially performing an informal but no less important research and development division for the recorded music industry. The location of Los Angeles, mainly the Hollywood area including and surrounding the Sunset Strip scene, contains the flux of ever-changing performers auditioning for a break. Contains, indeed. For it contains—as in, siphons off—this flux from the steadier parts of the business: the executive branches, the distribution, manufacturing, and marketing divisions of the companies.[2]

Geography plays an important role in focusing the flux and protecting the continuity of the dominant corporations. The travel costs, development costs (time spent on individual talent development and tryouts, group rehearsals, practices, rehearsal studio time, equipment), and performance costs (the running of a nightclub)—all, in this model, occur *outside* of the corporation, before any real investment in the creative product: the signing of an act and production of a record.

In this way, geography helps to tie some of the looser relationships together and, at the same time, to sustain their contingent status (a relationship could change—between a songwriter and a publisher or an artist and a producer—depending on evolving trends). Locating this activity—the search for new songs or artists—in a central place helps to organize this side of the business. And it explains how Los Angeles developed as a powerful hub in the 1960s pop music industry. One side of the system remained stable and strongly linked to relatively long-standing corporate headquarters, while the search for and discovery of talent, a fluctuating and shifting process, bubbled up in places like Los Angeles (or, for that matter, Nashville).

This kind of success, based on proximity, fed the soil, fertilizing the crops and growing land of the music industry and, in turn, drawing more talent, more grist for the maw. This migration itself enhanced the symbolism of Hollywood as a place for the music industry; in this sense, site and symbolism surged and reinforced one another. The agglomeration of economic and artistic practices grew deeper and more rooted. The influx of musicians streamed opportunities to the different levels of the city's—and its key industry's—ecosystem. Aspiring songwriters or artists evolved into session musicians; session musicians grew into back-up musicians for touring groups or local clubs, or worked as music teachers or in instrument sales or any of the many ancillary jobs servicing the area. The ecology shifted and expanded.

The Monkees leapfrogged most if not all these processes. Management signed the band basically before they even had a band, when it was just a concept. Then they put together the songwriters, producers, and musicians for the recordings. No clubs to test out their appeal. No word of mouth to draw in scouts or executives. Still, the hidden talent—Boyce and Hart and other songwriters, the session musicians, and engineers—worked their way through the city's networks and the connections in the music industry, proving their mettle. The Monkees drew on a team of preselected writers, already vetted and signed to Screen Gems-Columbia, and musicians with track records in studio sessions.

The Monkees project sprang from the genius of this system, the way it had been honed and streamlined into the important elements that contribute to a successful song. A publisher with an ear for hits. Songwriters hired by the publisher (and rewarded with a salary). The producers and studio musicians—the best of the best—translating those songs into their final form. The marketing and advertising supporting the distribution networks to get the song in front of audiences and with the right framework to shape its reception. And the genius of this system was hosted in a very specific and concrete geographic space: Hollywood, USA. When Schneider and Rafelson cooked up the laboratory experiment soon named the Monkees, they could do so with the confidence that a system existed, one in their own locale. All it needed was harnessing and links.

By how much did the Monkees skip the line? How many aspiring bands did the Monkees cut ahead of? No exact number offers itself up neatly since so many aspiring musicians or bands slip in and out of the system at different levels—high school dances, local bars and clubs, county fairs, amateur nights. Should we count all the kids playing songs in their room dreaming of fame but never fronting a public forum? Or the neighborhood groups jamming on cover songs in their garage? Probably not. But some numbers offer themselves up as a form of measurement. In pondering just this question, the sociologist Paul Hirsch had the ingenious idea to count two nationwide contests in 1967 for aspiring rock groups as a good estimate of potential "undiscovered" artists. One contest had 11,000 groups and 2,000 battled it out in another.[3] By this calculus, then, the Monkees jumped 13,000 spaces in line to land their recording contract. No dues or debts. No clubs or gigs; hey hey they're the Monkees.

Take another walk or trip through Hollywood in the 1960s and its musical ecosystem: the path of the Byrds. Their flight involved managerial manipulations at almost every stage of their development, if a little less so than the machine manufacturing of the Monkees. Still, their eventual manager tapped into real gatekeeping functions that were laced throughout LA's music industry and its geographic network. Like the Monkees, their story shows the strong power of local support. Moreover, their origin story maps out on the Hollywood music industry's geographic roots and it syncs up to the levels of the industrial system of recorded pop music.[4]

The members of the Byrds came together through Hollywood's clubs and a producer—management—who supported and strengthened these evolving relationships. Jim Dickson, a jazz producer curious about the folk music scene, met David Crosby, an eventual Byrd, at the Unicorn club on Sunset. Crosby earlier had met his soon-to-be bandmates Jim McGuinn and Gene Clark right around the corner at the Troubadour; their initial bonds grew through a love of folk and the Beatles. Since bands like the Modern Folk Quartet, the Kingston Trio, and others swirled through the LA scene, folk clubs like the Troubadour found agents, record company executives, and producers (like Dickson) crawling through the crowds, checking out the latest folk acts as potential pop hits.

Dickson managed this early trio's—Crosby, McGuinn, and Clark—initial stab at replicating the Beatles, when they went by the achingly Anglophile angle of the Beefeaters performing folksy pop in the mop-top vein. Their next steps gained from Dickson's intervention; in addition to bringing in bassist Chris Hillman, he called in a favor to a connection at the World Pacific Records recording studio on Santa Monica Boulevard, enabling him to use the grounds as a rehearsal space. Dickson thus exploited connections and relations that led from one to another in this very specific geographic place, as the clubs entertained "folk and roll" repertoires and record executives began to take an interest in the genre.

Dickson also managed to nab an early demo of Bob Dylan's "Mr. Tambourine Man" and conceived of it and this little embryonic egg of a band (the Byrds) as a marriage between the folk tune and the jangly sound of the British Invasion, or, more particularly, the Beatles. In doing so, Dickson acted just like a classic "A&R man," the old moniker of label executives employed by the record companies to match their contracted artists ("A" for artists) with the right material ("R" for repertoire), a management position that curated an artist's career. A&R men mostly disappeared in the pop era in the wake of singer-songwriters developing their own material. More accurately, the position just morphed into creative decisions made by record company executives, producers, and managers. If songwriters performed their own material in the pop era, the A&R logic surfaced in decisions about what material to include on an album, or what kinds of songs or genres would enhance, advance, or stall an artist's career. In this case, Dickson served the same function in the system, and his decision generated a sonic boom in the soundscape of the pop scene in Los Angeles (and, of course, this band's brief career).

Dickson's enthusiasm tipped off Columbia's interest in the band, who supported the production of a single to test out their commercial durability. Columbia assigned the band's production to their West Coast producer and talent scout Terry Melcher, a native Angeleno and part of the Hollywood caste system (he was Doris Day's son). Melcher tried a run as a singer but soon discovered an aptitude for producing, spinning out successful surf-rock albums and eventually tracks by Paul Revere and the Raiders (also signed to Columbia). When Melcher heard the Byrds, he found the ragtag band entirely lacking in real chops and called in sturdy session musicians for the first recordings: drummer Hal Blaine, bassist Larry Knechtel, Leon Russell on electric piano, and Jerry Cole on rhythm guitar, all of whom had worked with Melcher before (insider local connections paid the bills yet again).

Melcher strung the song together by foregrounding the shimmering chime of the 12-string electric guitar. In fact, Dickson had already produced an album featuring the 12-string guitar with Glen Campbell, and strongly considered bringing in Campbell to the Byrds' sessions (he was finally convinced that McGuinn could handle the instrument). Melcher enhanced the guitar with triple reverb effects, achieving the jangly sound that would distinguish this recording from folk-pop and other covers of Dylan's work. Melcher also had the idea to up the tempo of Dylan's number, modelling it on the Beach Boys' "Don't Worry Baby." You can hear the guitar treble chirp from the Beach Boys' song lifted directly onto Melcher's "Mr. Tambourine Man." You can also hear Melcher advising the band—on bootleg recordings—on the rhythm, pushing them to increase the tempo ever so slightly ("by a hair" or "play like you're all the lead") on take after take.

With the single primed for release, Dickson then arranged for the Byrds to play at Ciro's on Sunset Boulevard. In other words, the Byrds had a single, backed by studio musicians, ready for release before they played their first live shows together as a band. In their first shows, they stumbled through their sets awkwardly in front of small crowds. By the following week they had lines at the door, and by the end of the month their shows became a trendy spot for the Sunset Strip in-crowd, as the single flew up the Top 40 jet stream.

The formation of the Byrds neatly distills the ways artists rely on an art world to support their artistic productions—and how this process develops in the embedded social relations of the industry's systemic operations and its geographic boundaries. Dickson held links to World Pacific through his previous job there as an executive,

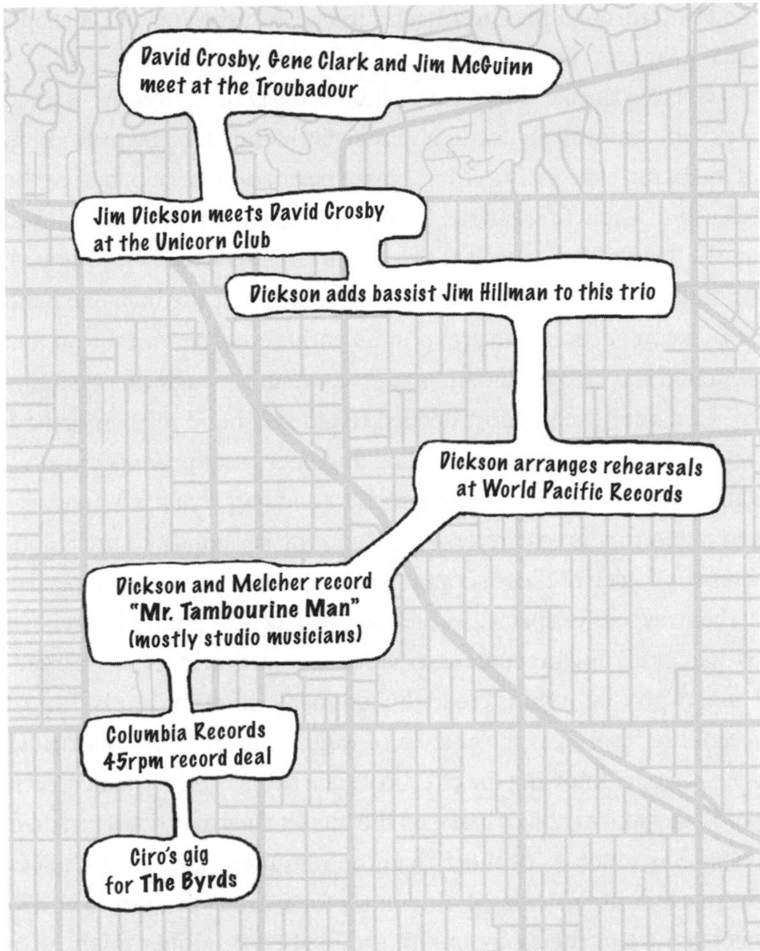

Jim Dickson discovers and steers the Byrds through their first flight in Los Angeles. Their first performances occur alongside their first recorded release, a twist on the typical gatekeeping path.

and this relationship gave him access to the studio to host the Byrds' early rehearsals and recordings. He scouted the Hollywood nightclubs out of an earnest and commercial curiosity regarding the new pop-folk scene. Likewise, Dickson exploited his relationship with Columbia's promotions team to obtain the acetate of Dylan's song. The cultural symbolism of Dylan, shared by the social scene radiating through the Los Angeles music industry, made Dickson's pitch a smart one.

Getting the band into Ciro's involved a transaction that served the club (to fulfill an evening's entertainment) and the promotion of the band, especially as a legitimate performing group, before the release of their first single. Local radio stations like KRLA picked up the single and soon it took off into the stratosphere, buoyed, no doubt, by Columbia's promotional team. But the invisible hand of Dickson secured the group in its early tentative formation and switched the latches and links to steer them through this system.

Consider the support needed to aid any band in their artistic practice. It ranges from recording engineers and producers, songwriters and musicians to photographers and hair stylists to designers and piano tuners to caterers (for recording sessions and press conferences). Each of these support personnel carry a level of expertise in their respective specialties and varying levels of reputation related to their skills and previous associations (commercial or artistic success). A producer gains credibility on many different levels, from a recent hit, from a particular style, or wedding an artist to a particular song or style. Knowing the effects of such decisions on their careers, producers make choices based on the impact they may render to their résumé as much as or more than the remuneration. Such choices fluctuate or are calculated differently for various producers at distinct points in their careers. An established producer might turn down an offer because it does little for their career in terms of reputation or even risks ruining it, despite substantial financial reward. In other words, a producer offers a judgment on a project as much as a cost.

Since so many of these support networks and contributions register as an investment, they operate, in varying degrees of magnitude, as gatekeeping functions, as assessments or evaluations. In other words, an artist's rise to prominence or exposure can occur before the instant of discovery or the momentous signing of a record company contract. That moment when a record company opens (or closes) the gate to an artist stands out as a significant and symbolic entry to their artistic expression and potential success. But gatekeepers function all over and at all levels of the industry—like interlocking canals—and they overlap significantly with all the specialists and supporters enumerated above. So, getting booked at a minor club represents an accomplishment, or approval from a minor gatekeeper. It registers as an achievement because the club owner recognizes some level of talent and opens the artist to other potential gatekeepers. Club owners might share their evaluation of the artist with a talent scout (an agent, manager, or A&R man). Or any of these gatekeepers might check out their show, based on word of mouth or a critic's review (another form of gatekeeping). A manager might sign the band and risk the free time invested in their promotion against a future payoff (10 percent of their eventual income). This commitment represents another acknowledgment, another clearance, another test passed, another gatekeeping function. How much so depends partly on the reputation of the manager. But even then, more hurdles remain. A reputable manager can open more doors more quickly, get calls returned, recordings listened to, and auditions arranged with speed and alacrity, but the record executives remain fully aware of the uncertainty of the market or the fact that even an established hitter sometimes strikes out.

In other words, it means something when a producer chooses to work with an artist; it's a sign to others, and other gatekeepers, in the industry. Other gatekeepers pay attention to these signs because they offer a degree of knowledge or faith that they themselves may bank on. Knowing that a respected producer collaborated with or a manager backed an artist might convince a DJ to gamble on a record.

This kind of "knowledge" circulates swiftly and efficiently in a city, a hub of cultural circuits. Informal exchanges come through musicians working on a production, tipping off others in an after-work rendezvous at a nightclub or other studio sessions with a different mix of musicians. Since the reception of a song, album, or performance remains ultimately uncertain, these informal exchanges remain as important and vital as more formal evaluations (a talent scout's assessment or a record company audition). So, proximity to the action—clubs, recording studios—is vital to the performance of competitors. It helps them sus out what is happening, what is potentially novel, and what they might be up against in climbing the charts and luring in listeners (consumers). In LA, the circuit of information exchange charged through the Sunset Strip clubs, coffeehouses, and studios from the Whisky to Ciro's to Gold Star.

These circuits of exchange and gatekeeping offer creative industries all kinds of mechanisms to increase the odds of success. Relying on conventions and previous hits offers a degree of prediction and protection. But, of course, conventions only carry so much assurance. Creative products must also by definition offer some element of novelty, of originality: each one must offer some distinction or newness. A slavish imitation of a previous hit might sustain some early interest (or none, you never know). But it risks overfamiliarity or indistinction if it sounds too much like another work.

Gatekeepers offer a way of testing out artists at an economy of scale. In the case of LA's music scene, nightclubs acted as an ecosystem; they were outside the administration of the recording industry, but served a function within the overall system. A live performance of a new song can test out its appeal with a small crowd, while satisfying the immediate performance contract of an evening's entertainment at a club. The damage done by a flat new song remains low so long as the performer delivers the club some entertainment. A bad show only lasts a night, and the club persists. The record company scout, meanwhile, can pluck a promising performer from this space and begin the path of stronger investment and increasingly greater risk. A low-cost single can score with a local DJ before a major label picks it up or radio stations in bigger markets add it to their playlists.

The ancillary practices—club gigs, independent labels—subsist on their limited scale and profit margins. And on the promise of feeding into the bigger hub: the major labels. The labels and each ring of the circle radiating outward rely on degrees of knowledge—a talent scout, a club owner, club crowds, a local DJ—to evaluate and anticipate the reception of these creative products, and to mitigate the certain risk entailed in a creative economy. At each level, decisions get made involving some scale of economic commitment. At some point, an act passes up all the rungs and the scale of support from the company gets stacked to a major level: recording costs, national distribution and promotion, advances on a follow-up record, tour support, and publicity.

The Monkees project involved harnessing all these different components of the system and its ecosystems from the start. In other words, it mapped out the connections while bypassing most of the distinct gatekeeping steps and functions. Before the individual members even auditioned, the management worked out what normally came in stages for other acts: the commitment to recording a single and an album, promotion to radio, a TV show, and possible live concerts (at least in concept or theory). Not every contract necessarily got signed in advance, but they laid down plans to develop these productions for the band. Even in the case of the Byrds, with all the advice and assistance afforded them by managers and producers, the band went through different stages to "audition" as individuals and as a group. In the case of the Monkees, the producers and management committed to the momentum from day one. In keeping with the picture we're painting of this system, each of the participants brought their own goals to the project, even as they shared the goals in each discrete stage of the project: putting on a TV show, releasing hit singles and albums, crafting the band's image, promoting the band, and putting on a concert tour.

For Bert Schneider and Bob Rafelson, the Monkees project meant using the television show to establish their credentials in crafting visual narratives, a track that might lead them to feature films, their long-term ambition. They said it was easier at this stage in their career to pitch a TV show than make a feature film, but they clearly saw it as a stepping stone, even if they authentically shared the youthful energy and spirit of the show and the whole project. For all of Schneider's entitled position—the son of the head of Columbia Pictures Television—the practice of gatekeeping still applied, as some chance still existed that the pilot would not fly.

Still, Schneider and Rafelson remained genuinely committed to the symbolic dimensions of the show and the way it resonated with camp, Pop art, the youth culture, and the counterculture. They knew what they were selling, but they also embraced the spirit of their objects of appropriation. These values need acknowledgment as well in the way they served to string together aspects of the show, from the costumes, insolent one-liners, and jump-cut editing, and most

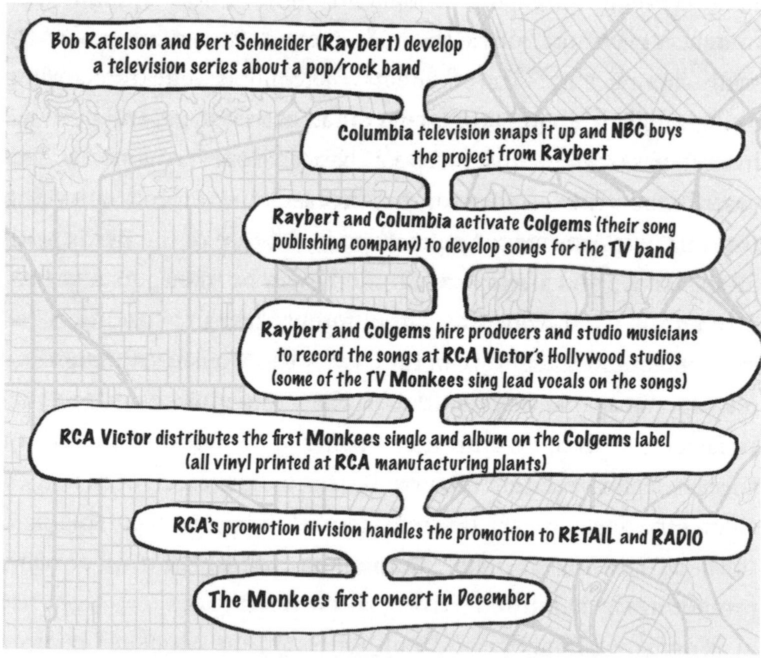

The Monkees bypass most of the gatekeeping mechanisms.

importantly to the music. If craftspeople like the film editors didn't share those values, they at least understood them, and this communication served as a way to bind the project together. Drawing from the Beatles and the spirit of pop music helped to sell the concept of the show and served as a template for the music, of course, but also for contributors like hairstylists and costume designers.

The relationship between Columbia's music divisions, with its publishing and record branches, was immediately galvanized by the Monkees project and put to work. In other words, Columbia could energize this conduit to its system of media alliances to service this production. Don Kirshner, the New York-based head of the Monkees' record label, operated in the inner grooves of the spiraling system supporting the project. Others, mainly the project's creators, Rafelson and Schneider, spun everything into motion. But Kirshner—or, initially, Kirshner's office—managed the musical component, and as that element grew in significance, soon overtaking other parts of the enterprise, Kirshner's oversight and influence grew. Kirshner established his business—contracting songwriters and negotiating recorded versions of their work—long before the Monkees project synched up with it. Moreover, he did so in New York, demonstrating the reach of media networking in the system of the American music business. His contributions—his stable of songwriters, his office's selection of material, and management of the recording process—skyrocketed the success of the whole Monkee business, in a way no other aspect of the system—public relations, television scriptwriters, studio musicians—can lay claim to. Yet, when the Monkees project launched in 1965, when it got the green light from Columbia's television executives, no one, not even Kirshner, knew the role his publishing company would play in the operation. The system established the connection. Only the system knew. Genius.

At the earliest stage of his career, Kirshner possessed a systematic mind and quickly established a publishing company after deciding to pursue a career in the music business.[5] He had fallen in love with music and musicians after finishing his college business degree and formed a songwriting partnership in 1955 with his childhood friend and rising singer Bobby Darin. Darin went on to success as a performer and songwriter on his own, leaving Kirshner with at least some knowledge of the ins and outs of the business—mostly the outs, as their songwriting efforts went nowhere.

On learning the "ins" as his songwriting efforts fell "out," Kirshner composed a new plan to get into the publishing end of the business. Kirshner recognized the incredible growth of pop and rock music in the late 1950s and the demand for material from the record companies as they sought to capitalize on this new trend. So, in 1958, Kirshner formed a publishing company with Al Nevins, a music business veteran with a background in songwriting, performing, and publishing—a shrewd move for young Kirshner as Nevins proved a mentor as much as a business partner. Kirshner returned the favor by bringing Nevins into the world of pop and rock, effectively modernizing his career. Al and Don christened their enterprise Aldon Music and set up shop in New York at 1650 Broadway, across the street from the Brill Building, a legendary hub for music publishers.

But the savviest move on Kirshner's part was his idea of systemizing the whole publishing operation by contracting songwriters as exclusive contributors to Aldon. In other words, Kirshner signed writers to the company in advance of any songs they would produce. Rather than buying or rejecting songs as writers came in to pitch them on a one-off basis by audition, the standard model of the times, Kirshner offered salaries to writers if they signed on the line, committing their work to the company in return for promised promotion: getting artists to record and release their work and the resulting royalties. A system. A mini system. One that served the bigger system of performers and record companies looking for material to fill their recordings and fulfill the promise of success on the radio and retail end of the system.

In this way, Aldon Music established an organizational structure from the start to gain and maintain their market position. It provided a framework of specialization and even standardization for the creation of this expressive art form—popular songs—that streamlined part of the process of production, creating and pitching songs to artists and record companies. Kirshner's company gave rock and pop an aura of craft and professionalism that enhanced the work of the composers who responded with hit after hit. Aldon offered songwriters a guaranteed income, a weekly salary (typically $50 to $150), against future song royalties in exchange for exclusive rights to their work. Thus, writers earned a moderate income while waiting for returns on the sales of their song. Aldon still split the royalty rate by the publishing standard at 50/50, so a penny each—to the publisher and the songwriters, respectively—for the sale of a song. Aldon then deducted their salary payments at any point from the writer's royalty check. The royalties on a hit song, however, could stack up, amounting to something like a conventional annuity for hit songwriters. Indeed, the bulk of Aldon's earnings came from a handful of songwriters. Thus, Aldon's system spread the risk of the salaries among the writers, since just a few major hits would cover the costs.

Take Jack Keller's 1959 Aldon contract as an explication of the logic of this system.[6] The reasoning and gamble behind this arrangement played out as follows: for a salary of $10,000 per year, Keller would give Aldon the exclusive publishing rights to his songs. For Keller, the arrangement promised him a conduit to getting his songs promoted and recorded, as well as the security of an income. Keller would still receive royalties from his songs, with Aldon recouping his salary from the total royalties. This provided an incentive to Aldon, in addition to their cut of the publishing royalties, to promote Keller's work since its success allowed them to recoup their salary payments.

Publishing companies, at this time, still operated in the tradition that established their formative role in the music industry:

namely, finding songwriters, signing them to their firm, and then soliciting performers to cover their songs (the publications) and getting them recorded.[7] By 1964 or so, more and more writers performed their own music, and, in these cases, publishers simply collected and accounted for the revenues for these artists, though they still shopped songs around (cover versions brought in additional revenue, after all). Writers needed the companies to confirm and maintain their copyrights on their songs and the flow of remuneration. The publishing company collected the revenue coming through BMI (Broadcast Music, Inc.) or ASCAP (the American Society of Composers, Authors, and Publishers), which tallied and collected payments from radio and other public performances of songs. As a new player in this field (founded in 1939), BMI had attracted many of the new pop and rock artists. Moreover, BMI offered subsidies and incentives to attract publishing firms to their organization, an overture Aldon took advantage of, using the subsidies as additional cash advances for their writers.

Kirshner curated songs and writers for his company by the standards of Top 40 radio—an immediate melodic hook to capture listeners (and radio programmers) of about two minutes in duration. He based these decisions on the template provided by previous hits and many of those in his catalogue. Kirshner's genius—his storied "Golden Ear," as a contemporary *Time* magazine profile dubbed his Midas lobes—lay in recognizing the potential of a song and of songwriters. Even while evaluating material, Kirshner took a systemic approach, compiling lists of songs organized around themes as a structure for coaching his writing staff.[8]

Early on, Kirshner demonstrated a knack for recognizing talent that translated into a string of signings and hits, a sensational streak of success racking up 54 Top 10 songs from 1960 to 1963. By 1962, Aldon managed eighteen writers on their staff, and created a few of their own record labels to broaden and deepen their revenue stream. Hitmakers like Neil Sedaka, Howard Greenfield, Jack Keller, Jerry

Don Kirshner's chartbusting squadron of songwriters.

Goffin, Carole King, Barry Mann, and Cynthia Weil. Kirshner and his team combined writers on songs, mixed up the pairs to generate different tunes, and supported and encouraged regular working partnerships. Soon these writers churned out major hits: "Will You Love Me Tomorrow," "Up on the Roof," "Dream Lover," "Uptown," "Breaking Up Is Hard to Do," "Calendar Girl," "Where the Boys Are," "I Love How You Love Me," "The Loco-Motion," "On Broadway," and "Take Good Care of My Baby."

Maintaining this company contributed to a sense of professionalization in the composition of pop songs. In turn, the writers evinced a level of respect for their work, and this translated into the formal command demonstrated by them. When the market indicated, they turned out novelty songs or silly camp like "Splish Splash," "Stupid Cupid," or "Let's Turkey Trot." Still, a sense of true craft unified compositions by different writers at Aldon. "Uptown" by Mann and Weil sketched an Ashcan social realism about a man living in a tenement and traveling to work every morning to face adversity but returning to live like a king with the song's narrator. "Crying in the Rain" slipped into a portrait of pain and withholding, slurring the tears with rainy weather. A similar impressionist narrative comes through in King and Goffin's "Up on the Roof," its lyrics playing with up and down as measures of the cityscape, buildings, crowds, and solace, and as descriptions of moods, then folding this latter emotional inflection with the urban space of the streets and rooftops.

In a significant way, Aldon's organizational logic here anticipated the work Kirshner and his team would perform for the Monkees. They brought the same conceptual process governing the creation of songs. As they did at Aldon, for the Monkees Kirshner and his writers tailored their work to the artistic specifications and genre conventions informing the project. They studied the market and the art form, and matched writers and musicians for the recordings. The music-made-to-order model matched the Monkees machine.

With West Coast producers like Phil Spector and Snuff Garrett jetting in and out of his East Coast office, Kirshner picked up on the Pacific winds. Aldon Music opened a West Coast office in 1961, a clear recognition of LA's growing significance in the pop and rock market. Kirshner hired Lou Adler to lead their Hollywood outpost, a savvy choice since Adler occupied courtside seats in LA's exploding music scene, managing Jan and Dean, writing songs for Sam Cooke, and eventually founding Dunhill Records after leaving Aldon in 1963. Moreover, Adler brought the West Coast sound to Aldon, signing writers like P. F. Sloan and Steve Barri to the firm.

Two years later, in a seismic move, Kirshner sold Aldon Music outright—including its catalog of copyrights—to Columbia Pictures in April 1963 for $2 million worth of the movie studio's stock (according to Kirshner, Bert Schneider drove the pursuit by Columbia). Kirshner became president of the music division—renamed Screen Gems-Columbia Music Inc.—including the publishing wing and struggling Colpix record label (a more attuned accounting put the sale in figures of a little over a million plus stock, but stock fluctuations make it difficult to put a precise number on the overall sale, so $2 million stands as a good representative figure). Savvier yet, Kirshner convinced most of his songwriting teams at Aldon to sign with the new company. That move, a gambit put in motion by the system, anticipated synergy between the two businesses, something that played out immediately in the theme songs for TV shows like *Bewitched*, *Gidget*, and *I Dream of Jeannie*, composed by former Aldon songwriters induced to join the purchase. Kirshner, in fact, held a music supervisor credit on the programs and planted some of his firm's songwriters like Boyce and Hart in guest appearances on the shows.

Long before the Monkees project even germinated, then, the system established a connection between divisions of song publishing, recording, and television. The Monkees project only activated these preexisting links, fulfilling the promise anticipated in the initial deal. In other words, the players at the time of the Monkees project's origins—Kirshner's office, Raybert's management, and the exclusively employed songwriters—availed themselves of the networks already engineered within the system. Indeed, Kirshner initially only managed these links from a distance, remaining in his New York office throughout 1965 and early 1966, as he did with his supervising role over other television shows and their music. However, in June 1966, Columbia Pictures announced the formation of Colgems, a label primarily devoted to releasing recordings by the Monkees, with distribution from RCA Victor. They placed Kirshner in the president's role. Moreover, RCA agreed to fund the Monkees' recording sessions, committing to annual advances of $40,000 to cover the costs. Since most recordings occurred in RCA-owned studios (as well as using RCA-manufactured magnetic sound tape and equipment), most of these costs remained in-house, all deductible as recoupable costs before any royalties went out to any talent. Contracted calculations like these were standard in the business and mitigated the risks for the labels in releasing new music.

Behind Kirshner, yet another system. For Kirshner commissioned Lester Sill to oversee Aldon's—or by now Colgems'—operations in their Los Angeles office. A native Angeleno, Sill grew up with and in the city's growing music industry. He worked his way from nightclubs to production, guiding sessions on early recordings of material by the early rockers Leiber and Stoller, even establishing a small record company with the rock legends. When the label got picked up by Atlantic, Sill became its national sales manager while simultaneously managing its big act, the Coasters. Even so, Sill spun out other record labels, produced twangy early hits from Duane Eddy, and soon got involved with Phil Spector, with the two forming their own successful label to support Spector's phenomenal hits like "He's a Rebel," "Then He Kissed Me," and "Be My Baby" (evidently a maestro of fleecing as much as producing, Spector squeezed Sill out of the company). When he landed at Screen Gems, Sill brought deep cuts of experience to what he considered a temporary position while he weighed other prospects. The immediate success of the Monkees solidified Sill's supervisory role and drew on his experience as a label owner, a producer, a guiding force in song selection and managing crews for recordings.

In supervising the Monkees' productions on the West Coast, Sill collaborated heavily with another Colgems employee: signed songwriter and occasional producer Jack Keller. At Aldon, while Keller knocked out songs like "Everybody's Somebody's Fool" and "My Heart Has a Mind of Its Own" (both hits for Connie Francis), he also became a deft handler of the recording and engineering process, getting to know the knobs and buttons on the consoles and more than capable of directing the performances, bringing out the singers or musicians at the right pitch and pace.

Keller's inroads into other aspects of music production beyond his songwriting endeavors were covered and encouraged in his

Performing for Number One: songwriters Tommy Boyce and Bobby Hart audition a number for their boss Don Kirshner.

contract with Aldon as it promised "to counsel [Jack Keller] as to contracts for his professional work . . . [and] . . . to make the professional career of [Keller] the success contemplated, both professionally and financially." Thus, when the Hollywood market began to take off for Keller, mostly in the form of television theme songs, Keller took to the coast with Aldon's encouragement. Keller's composition (cowritten with Howard Greenfield) for *Bewitched* won over the show's producers and even became a Top 10 radio hit with a version by Billy Costa.

Once in Los Angeles, Keller became a regular collaborator and advisor to Lester Sill in work on Aldon projects. Thus, when Keller landed in the recording booth for the first sessions of the Monkees, the system had already put the scaffolding into place, since Keller had worked for the company since 1959. Indeed, in 1966, Colgems tendered a new contract to Keller expressly for the purpose of guiding the Monkees through their first recordings. It noted that "from time to time during the term hereof we may elect to engage you to render your services as a producer" for the Monkees. The contract

Lester Sill and Jim Keller supervising a Monkees recording session.

clarified the organizational structure behind Keller's contributions to the Monkees: "Your services rendered pursuant to this agreement shall be subject to the supervision and direction of the Director of Popular Artist and Repertoire . . . or a person designated by him," which referred to Kirshner or Sill. That meant Keller had to discuss the concept, repertoire, arrangements, and accompaniments for any Monkees recording (the song choice, the instrumentation, and the production) with Kirshner or Sill. But though they baked this process into the contract, the decisions were made in the studio and on the fly. Few if any meetings belabored this point; this contract clause only clarified the ultimate decisions regarding which tracks would get released and who held sway over the choices. Everyone understood the guiding principles—pop rock and Top 40 radio—behind the recordings. For his services as producer, Keller received a standard of 2 percent of the retail returns on the records. The contract designated Keller as a co-producer with Boyce and Hart on the following songs:

"I'll Be True to You"
"Theme from the Monkees"
"Saturday's Child"
"Take a Giant Step"
"This Just Doesn't Seem to Be My Day"
"Let's Dance On"

And as a co-producer with Jeff Barry on "Your Auntie Grizelda" (a Keller composition that would show up on the band's second album). Keller's primary task involved helping Boyce and Hart figure out their roles as producers, in addition to advising on the arrangements.

Initially, Kirshner hired Snuff Garrett, an experienced craftsman in pop recordings on works by Gary Lewis and the Playboys, Bobby Vee, Del Shannon, and others, to supervise the music production. But Garrett walked away after experiencing the band and its very evident amateurism in its initial recordings. The snub by Snuff—followed quickly by other rejections from Mickie Most (producer for the Animals and Herman's Hermits) and Goffin and King—represented a minor gatekeeping statement. Ordinarily a rejection by such a tastemaker might signal some potential trouble on a project. But this enterprise had the whole narrative predetermined more or less: a single had to accompany the initial promotion and exploitation of the show. The recordings and TV show would reinforce each other.

By default, then, Boyce and Hart ended up in the producer's chair (with Keller's assistance) and pushed through the recording sessions in the summer and fall of 1966, leading up to the TV show's debut and its tie to the first single and album. Garrett's refusal led to their first effort at producing—indeed, producing their own material—and calling in their crew of studio musicians. Boyce and Hart passed through the internal gate or filter by producing a song that Kirshner picked as the first release for the Monkees project. "Clarksville" fit the bill in terms of the standards of pop-rock at this crossroads in the late summer of 1966. It had a British Invasion vibe. The riff sounded like the Stones' "The Last Time" (a similar descent in melody, a hand-clapping sing-along quality, and the same beat) or the Beatles' "Run for Your Life" (same note progression, more or less, on the riff). Granted, by 1966, many other artists were moving on from this rockabilly-skittle, folk and roll sound. Regardless, it fit right in with other contenders on the charts. In short, Boyce and Hart nailed it, as did the back-up band of studio musicians, the complementary studio engineering of RCA's recording engineer Dave Hassinger, and Micky Dolenz's exuberant vocal performance.

The campaign to radio stations—and, of course, the repeated use of the song in early episodes of the TV show—built on the momentum of the RCA Victor machine. It remains difficult to measure the contributions of radio enthusiasm, the commentaries of tip sheets like the *Gavin Report* or similarly functional columns in *Cashbox*, *Radio and Records*, and *Billboard* encouraging stations to consider the song for their playlists, and the expensive campaign RCA Victor lent to the release of the song. Difficult to measure precisely but weighing in the contributions of this campaign certainly adds up to something that tips the scale, especially when compared to other equally great songs. The system—RCA's promotion and distribution infrastructure, and the Raybert team's brilliant idea to wed musical releases to national television exposure—took the song to a whole other level of exposure.

For RCA promised and delivered on a $100,000 campaign to support the single's release, reportedly sending 76 promotors across the country to sell the song to radio and retail (the reports come

Hey, hey: in-store promotional displays supplied by RCA Victor, the major monopoly behind the Monkees record releases.

from publicity releases to trade papers, and the number tallies with promoters already regionally employed for the firm). RCA hit DJs with teaser ads and a newspaper-type brochure with pictures and biographical stories on the Monkees. Retail stores—through RCA's promotors and distributors—received ad mats, four-color centerpiece displays, window displays, and point-of-sale materials, including blanket mats and miniatures, advertising the single, the band, and the forthcoming TV show and album.

While Colgems represented a new independent label, it remained only nominally so as it functioned entirely as a platform for the Monkees' releases under the auspices of a true juggernaut: RCA Victor. In other words, Colgems faced none of the other obstacles of a true independent: risking its collateral on the hit or miss of an artist or finding the means to capitalize on a hit on a national level by attempting to contract with independent distributors without the clout of a back catalog or promotional campaign. When Colgems released "Last Train to Clarksville" and soon after the Monkees' first album, and then the follow-up smash single "I'm a Believer," it did so through the already established RCA Victor promotion and distribution network. So when Colgems launched its national campaign pushing the Monkees to radio stations, it could bank on the fact that RCA's promotion and distribution infrastructure supplied local retail outlets with the single when radio play stimulated sales, and vice versa—as John Rosica, RCA Victor's National Sales and Promotion manager, affirmed to a convention of the company's regional distributors and promoters: "You cannot hope to or be expected to put every single release into your one-stops and major dealers. *But* we do expect you to put out the records that get (air) play."[9] For most of these regional distributors, promotion, including campaigns directed at their local radio stations, went hand in hand with promotion at the retail level. RCA Victor possessed an established national network that bolstered such campaigns, a system covering the United States:

RCA Distributors, Inc.	Albany, NY
RCA Victor Distributing Corp.	Atlanta, GA
Interstate Distributing Company	Billings, MT
Eastco, Inc.	Cambridge, MA
Southern Radio Corp.	Charlotte, NC
D&H Distributing Co.	Cheverly, MD
Ohio Appliances, Inc.	Cincinnati, OH
Main Line Cleveland, Inc.	Cleveland, OH
CALECTRON	Daly City, CA
Adleta Company, Inc.	Dallas, TX
Ward Terry & Company	Denver, CO
Sea Coast Appliance Distributors	Hialeah, FL
Radio-TV Corp, RCA Victor	Honolulu, HI
Art Jones & Company	Houston, TX
Associated Distributors	Indianapolis, IN
McClung & Co.	Knoxville, TN
RCA Victor Distributing Corp.	Los Angeles, CA
McDonald Brothers Company, Inc.	Memphis, TN
Taylor Electric Co.	Milwaukee, MN
McDonald Sales Corp.	New Orleans, LA
Bruno-New York, Inc.	New York, NY
Krich-New Jersey, Inc.	Newark, NJ
Dulany's	Oklahoma, OK
Sidles Company	Omaha, NE
Raymond Rosen & Co.	Philadelphia, PA
Hamburg Brothers, Inc.	Pittsburgh, PA
Commercial Distributors	Portland, ME
North Pacific Supply Co.	Portland, OR
Huish Distributing Co.	Salt Lake City, UT
Fidelity Northwest, Inc.	Seattle, WA
Interstate Supply Co. Record Division	St. Louis, MO
Morris Distributing Co.	Syracuse, NY
RCA Distributing Corp.	Shawnee Mission, KS
RCA Distributing Corp.	Taylor, MI[10]

These regional corporate outposts and distributors controlled or contracted by RCA ensured that the label's records would get stocked in stores, primed for purchase if the releases scored to varying degrees on radio and with audiences of consumers.

Moreover, these songs—a brilliant composition like "Last Train to Clarksville"—remained commodities as well. We can forget that, although it was played on the air for free, a song existed first on a piece of vinyl, a physical object that required possession for enjoyment at home, like a book or magazine. Therefore, it required physical distribution and boxing, shipping, transportation, unboxing, and display at the retail level in department stores, drug stores, and record stores (the dedicated handful popping up here and there across the land). RCA contracted with companies like McClung & Co. in Tennessee or the Adleta Company in Dallas, which supplied all kinds of retail products to stores in their regions, as well as their own RCA regional branches and promotional workers to ensure their product would find a retail space for consumers.

In many cases, the distributors simply placed the records in the retail stores on established RCA racks or in the store's retail bins with standard orders. In these cases, the store willingly relinquished selecting records for sale and trusted the regional distributor through RCA to stock the store with their latest release because it could return unsold product at no cost to the retailer. The availability on retail shelves, as in the case of "Last Train to Clarksville" and the Monkees' first album, ensured by powerful distribution systems like RCA, based on proven track records and relatively long-standing agreements and operations in regional markets, bolstered any song or artist that took off on radio. Artists that sustained similar airplay failed to sustain leaps to the next level of sales, at least on a national level, without such corporate infrastructural support. And, of course, sales triggered further airplay.

The quality and artistry of the Monkees' songs came from how different institutional forces—producers, song publishers, studio musicians—coordinated individual contributions in a fertile forum for creation. And they came from an art world with multiple contributions from different talented individuals, all supported and sustained by the cityscape of Los Angeles and its industrial institutions serving the music business.

Songwriters and producers like Boyce and Hart, the guitarist Louie Shelton, or writer and producer Jack Keller fused with the "style" of the Monkees and with its management structure, resources and infrastructure, and market strategy. And ultimately the style represented no more than an inspired inflection of an established style: the Monkees could have performed "I Got You Babe" or "Mr. Tambourine Man." Sonny Bono or Bob Dylan just weren't in their bank of songwriters.

Kirshner's systematic approach in his early publishing company anticipated the methods behind the Monkees' productions and the project itself. Kirshner's songwriters responded to the demands of the record company through the advice and mediation of their publishers and producers. This consultation occurred in discussions in the studio with the producers and in their contracts, which gave the right of selection and refusal to the publisher and producers. The same practices operated on the Monkees' productions, as Kirshner, the producers, and other executives like Lester Sill huddled together to debate and discuss with the contracted songwriters the most promising songs and recordings at their disposal. For the writers, this arrangement offered evaluation by the standards of the craft governing the pop industry that could inform their work. It focused the feedback process. At Aldon, the writers were fed tips from the song pluggers from the information they gleaned on routine meetings with producers and record executives. With the Monkees, the same process applied, only narrowed down to this production and its demands: pop music informed by the Beatles and the British Invasion. Kirshner's operation also spread the risk on the gamble. Other bands or artists gambled on a single writer or writing pair belonging to the act for follow-up hits or additional material, but here a string of hitmakers was available. If one well ran dry, they could gamble on another one. The

Monkees' production spread its bets, in favor of the house: the house Kirshner built.

Not one level of this structure retained a pure "genius," save perhaps for a couple of songwriters like Carole King or Neil Diamond. Each specialist brought their own skills to individual parts of the production: Kirshner's songwriters, Sill's supervision, Boyce and Hart, Keller's production work, the sharp professionalism of the musicians, RCA's sales force, and the leverage of its back catalog. When you tallied it all up, when you put together the whole equation, it resulted in a level of genius: sparkling and enduring songs like "Last Train to Clarksville," "Take a Giant Step," and "I'm a Believer."

4

State-of-the-Art Song System

The place: 7031 Woodrow Wilson Drive, Hollywood Hills. The time: summer of 1966. The space: interior of a car as it pulls into the carport. Bobby Hart, the driver, hits the KHJ button on the radio presets just in time to hear the closing section of the Beatles' "Paperback Writer" as it rolls and churns through its fade-out. Hart, a songwriter currently tasked with developing material for a brand-new fabricated-for-television band, the Monkees, parks the car and receives the radio waves; the tune fires the musical wires in his brain, only mistaking the lyrics for something about a train or a last train. Hart "figured the rest had to be something about a train to somewhere."[1]

The *mise-en-scène* flickers with Los Angeles totems. The car, as essential to LA living as a pair of shoes. The carport built into the housing, an architectural dwelling in its own right (domestic domicile for cars and their drivers). The car radio, so essential to the LA driving experience; KHJ, where "Paperback Writer" topped the local charts that same summer. Of course, the Beatles were everywhere in 1966, and everyone was trying to figure out their magic, no one more so than Bobby Hart. He retained a contract explicitly tasked to imitate the Beatles. That made this new Beatles song even more resonant for this driver. Finally, and most essentially, we find in this anecdote a scene of the working songsmith, always tuned in for sudden inspiration, and the bolt of revelation here enhanced by the utterly quotidian setting: a carport, and its sense of a fleeting moment—a song searing into his consciousness even as he only catches the fade.

The story captures aspects of a songwriter's working method: hearing or mishearing elements of another song and riffing on them to create something original, or a variation on that song. Writers sometimes take a song directly as a starting point to disassemble it, slow it down, or consciously rearrange it into something different. A song might gnaw at them—an intriguing chord change, a complex arrangement—rousing the writer to take the song apart like a mechanic to see how it works and then build a variation. Almost every songwriter speaks of such moments or practices. Or something very similar happens, in the way of Hart's story; scrambling the dial of their muse, searching for inspiration, a snippet zaps into their radar and they take it in and take it apart, poaching some pieces to rework in their own song.

Both variations of this process operate as challenges. Songwriters hear something intriguing or innovative, and this provocation spurs them on to figure out the formal elements at play and effectively assign themselves the task of figuring it out and working through it and with it. Hart acknowledges this practice. But, of course, his songwriting alarms went off because he had a mandate tied to this spontaneous sonic inspiration and its source: the Beatles. Hart had been hired to write songs in the style of the Beatles by the management team of the Monkees' productions. This instant in the carport, then, tapped a problem Hart lived with in the summer of 1966 and prompted a new direction, a fleeting set of elements to play with in building a new song in the vein of the Beatles. The inspirational moment occurred only because Hart was *tuned in*—tuned into the radio, and always tuned in to the currents of his art form's world. As a working songsmith, you had to be tuned in to the standard practices, the current conventions, and the latest developments.

Riffing off the initially misunderstood lyrics (Hart figured out the real lines, of course) to "Paperback Writer," he realized that

"Last Train" offered an intriguing motif for a song. His writing partner, Tommy Boyce, agreed, and they took off with it. "Last Train" captured a significant and subtle aspect of Beatles songs through its wistful ambiguity and impressionistic narrative. Even before the Beatles began their more experimental phase—before their discovery of Dylan and then going all eclectic on *Rubber Soul* and *Revolver*—their compositions traced more complex emotions than most pop songs. "I'll Follow the Sun," for example, offered a brusque portrait of a confused forlorn lover. Even a rousing pop song like "She Loves You" twisted the romance by framing the expressions through a friend consoling a girl and confirming her love to another friend—slightly more complex scenarios, acknowledging other relationships and emotional attachments, in comparison to "Chapel of Love," "Then He Kissed Me," or "Surfer Girl." "Paperback Writer" (and its flipside "Rain") built on these complex variations by completely abandoning any romantic themes. Paul frames the verse and chorus as a query letter from an author to a publisher. Then he even turns the story in on itself as the aspiring paperback writer's pitch gets revealed as a novel about an aspiring paperback writer.

An intriguing impressionist story line whistles through "Last Train" as well. The lyrics offer hints of a wistful narrative context as the narrator implores his lover to rush down to the titular town for what may be their last meeting. He has confidently (or obsessively) made a reservation on the train for his lover even before successfully convincing her to depart. Moreover, his timing suggests they'll spend the night together as his train departs the next morning. But the song conveys these elements of the story through elliptical phrases and scenes. The larger context—the urgency, the departure, the nature of the relationship—remains ambiguous.

So ambiguous, in fact, that some have claimed, with Boyce and Hart's occasional support, that the song depicts a young man about to be shipped off to Vietnam. Proponents of this interpretation point to a train station in Clarksville, Tennessee, near an army base as

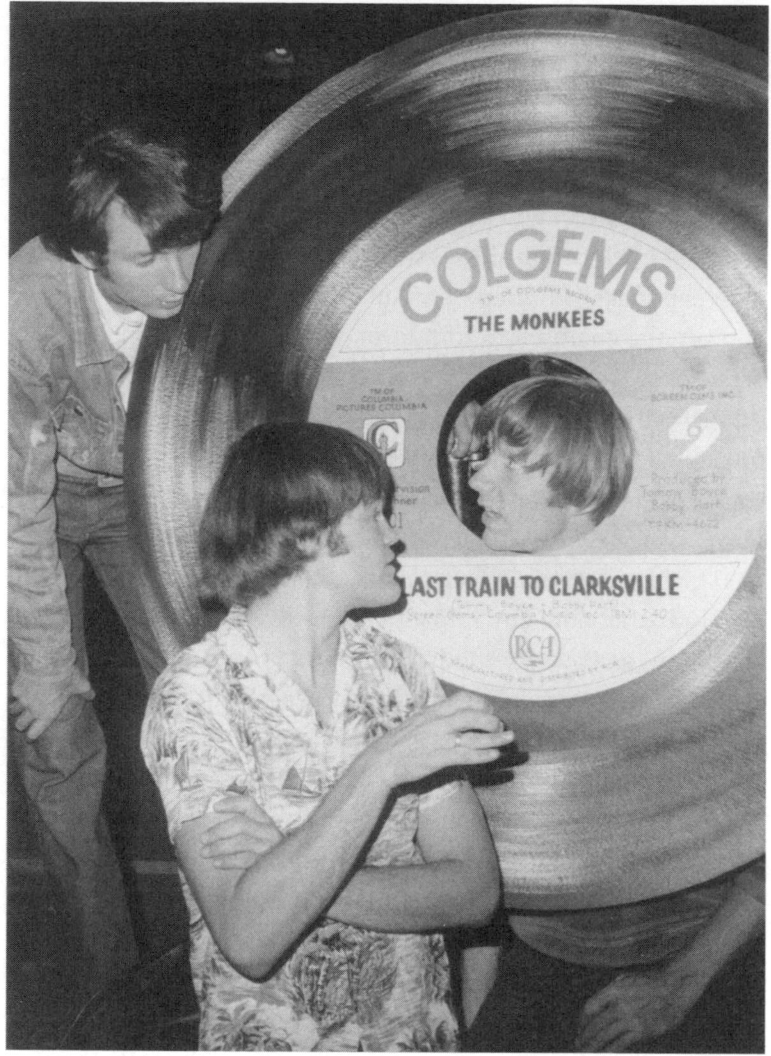

Monkees working on—or, rather, in—a record.

the song's reference. Hart encouraged this reading by slyly evoking self-censorship to explain away the lack of real support for such an interpretation. Yet in the same telling Hart notes that he and Boyce searched for a town name to fit the song's melodic line before he recalled the small town of Clarkdale near his hometown in Arizona, just twisting the name a bit for melodic effect. While the evocation of the Vietnam War remains a highly unlikely allusion in the song, such an interpretation confirms the song's ambiguity: the reader can fill in or speculate on its larger context or simply relish the ineffable yet clear emotional tones of the song. The potential fleeting romantic reunion comes replete with loss and melancholy. Like early Beatles pop, "Last Train" laces its romantic motifs with a sense of transitory time and urgency, qualities that resonate with teens in particular, whose crushes or relationships can always seem evanescent or fragile.

The airy melodic verse in "Last Train" operates within the same dynamic as its snappy Top 40-friendly opening hook. Both work through the range of notes in the G chord or scale that drives the song's first few measures. The guitar lick kicks through the G, F, E, and D notes, snapping on half beats, and dips into E and D notes on single strings, running through the steady beat on the G chord. The melody uses the dominant 7th of the G major scale and lands on that note (F) strongly (normally it would be the F-sharp), which firmly places the song in a rock melodic structure, apart from the jangly folk tone of the G chord. Your ear gets used to the F note, holding up there for a number of measures so that the drop to the C chord comes as a lilting release (Micky's resigned singing, releasing his breath with perfect timing, matches this release). Glistening, crystalline arpeggios on the guitar's treble strings signal the LA folk-rock tone sought out in the initial proposal for the band's sound (recall the original audition ad). The song's story line, a kind of ballad (a song that tells a story)—trains, small town, desperation—and its broad chord progression, jangly rhythm guitar, and simple I-IV bassline effectively evoke folk and fuse with a rock melodic line, ripping rock guitar lick, and twangy, trebly amplification. The string of "no's" sung by a chorus over the 7th chord might even represent an inverted wink to the "yeahs" that marked "She Loves You," and summed up the playful pop of the Beatles.

In its musical structure, then, "Last Train" echoes the form of "Paperback Writer," which also supports its lyrical verse on a single chord for several measures (eight in this case). Like "Paperback," as well, "Last Train" replaces a middle-eight (where a song shifts to a new chordal and melodic variation) with a suspension. Indeed, "Paperback" pays homage to the Beach Boys in this section, with the music dropping out completely as the lads layer harmonic choral repetitions of the song's title. In "Last Train," Boyce and Hart return the British inversion with Beatlesque suspension. The music drops out with only the guitar strumming two chords, every second beat for two measures, while Micky and the back-up singers (Boyce, Hart, Keller, et al.) repeat doo-do-doo-do. This section delivers another clear derivation from "Paperback" and an LA-British connection to the Beach Boys: the absorption of the British Invasion gets returned here to Southern California's shores. Likewise, the chiming guitar by session musician Gerry McGee and shimmering trebly arpeggios echo the LA-Beatles connection with its serene evocation of the Byrds or "Needles and Pins," the sounds of LA's "folk and roll." All these elements helped to make "Clarksville" a delectable pop song and—enhanced by the radio and TV promotion—a major hit, topping the charts and riding them all through the fall 1966 season (it certainly helped the band's first album reach No. 1 as well).

Flip over the "Clarksville" 45 and you find further evidence of the real distinction of this band: "Take a Giant Step" by pop songsmiths Goffin and King, leading contributors to Aldon and now Screen Gems-Columbia Music, another tune drawn from the publishing sources fueling the Monkees. Goffin and King could step backward in their history by noting that the Beatles, the current musical revolutionists shaking up the industry and culture, covered one of their songs—the brilliant pop-gospel "Chains"—and drew inspiration from the songwriting couple. Yet Goffin and King understood that the Beatles—along with Dylan, the Stones and a few others—shook up everyone's understanding of music and performance, in aesthetics and execution: the performers wrote their own genre-bending and -blending material. So, by 1965 and 1966, Goffin and King, these hit-making giants, found themselves in a similar position to the upstarts Boyce and Hart: playing catch-up. No less than Boyce and Hart, then, Goffin and King got to work studying the new sounds: the complexity of the lyrics, the clangy finger-picking riffs on guitars, the surprising chord shifts, and startling bridges and middle-eights. With songs like "Take a Giant Step," Goffin and King showed that they could follow in the footsteps of the Beatles.

The song opens with a guitar fillip that evokes Buddy Holly's guitar tricks absorbed by the Beatles and the Byrds. Yet, like the Beatles, Goffin and King seared these elements drawn from Holly and the Everly Brothers to the revved-up RPMs of Chuck Berry with its scrub brush guitar strumming and pumping bassline. The lyrics offer a minor twist on the typical romantic pop themes as the singer

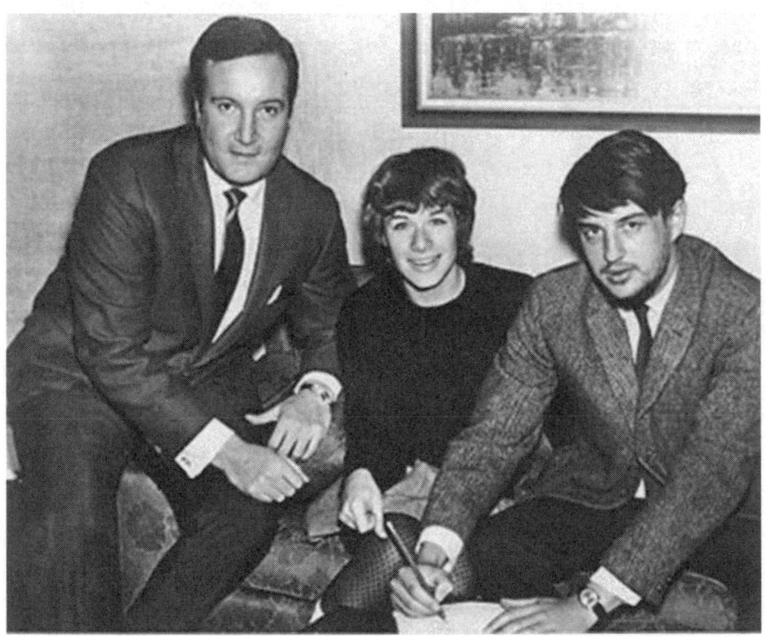

Goffin and King signed and resigned with Don Kirshner's stable of songwriters.

attempts to pull a potential lover out of their heartbreak from a previous relationship, though consolation as seduction admittedly presents a tried-and-true technique. In their production of the song, Boyce and Hart layered these elements with psychedelic touches rather like the Byrds and their variations on Dylan. The psychedelic raga vibe kind of falls apart near the end of the production, and despite the engineer's (Hank Cicalo) efforts, the final mix sounds a bit muddy, like some of the Stones' sessions.

What truly distinguished the Monkees comes out clearly on both sides of their first 45: songwriting teams signed to Screen Gems-Columbia Music. Boyce and Hart on one side, Goffin and King on the other: hitmakers on both sides and both under contract to the same publishing company mandated to deliver songs to the Monkees project. No other musical act at the time possessed such access, such a connection to a music machine. The songwriters worked under the same uncertainty dictating the market as any other writer and performer—no one really knows how audiences will respond to a creative work. Its appeal can only be determined when it gets released. Both sides of the 45, then, might not have played. But no other act had such resources at their disposal. Kirshner and his underlings—Lester Sill, Jack Keller, Boyce and Hart (in their capacity as producers)—sifted through dozens of potential songs, some put forward by their writers (as in the case of "Clarksville"), some already in the filing cabinet, so to speak (as in the case of "Steppin' Stone"), and evaluated their merits before committing them to the recording studio and then to release. In other words, a team of advisors, while no guarantors of success in a market as turbulent as pop, weighed the merits of songs against their understanding of the form and current tastes and trends. If one songwriting team failed to develop a song solid enough for release, the management team could survey other writers in their stable for stronger potential material. Moreover, they could advise songwriters, transforming or modulating a song to enhance its fit for the Monkees project.

Kirshner found "Clarksville," for example, too untraditional for a pop song since it lacked a clear romantic expression. But through his work with his team and their consultations with him, he understood the ways that the song reverberated with new pop trends, particularly those coming out of Los Angeles. Working with teams of writers—a factory?—meant more than following a single pop formula, since audience tastes shifted subtly and sometimes swiftly. A successful manager in this system, like Kirshner, remained flexible and responsive to the artists under his employ, and to new trends like the Beatles and the "folk and roll" sound of the West Coast.

One sign of the selection process that preceded the release of the Monkees' recordings comes in the AFM statements collected and perused by Andrew Sandoval in his day-by-day book on the band. The documents betray how many songs went through the recording process—sometimes with no vocals laid down by any of the Monkees—that failed to make the cut of a 45 or album release. Those documents only reveal the decision to proceed with the recording, therefore indicating an earlier process of consideration over other songs that failed to make it to this next step. Each step, then, amounts to a filtering by the team of creative advisors steering the project. Indeed, Boyce, Hart, Keller, and other producers logged so many recordings in 1966 that Kirshner and his team saved them for the second album, ready and waiting on the success (or failure) of the first.

One of the many miraculous facets of bands like the Beatles or the Stones remains their capacity to follow up hits with other hits. The fate of one-hit wonders or bands with a short string of hits like ? and the Mysterians or the Turtles testifies to the scarcity of enduring pop acts. The uncertainty of audience reactions would make it difficult to argue that the Monkees project solved this problem through its reliance on a stable of successful songwriters, most of whom had a proven track record of hits. However, Kirshner and his team certainly addressed the problem of material and did so in a systematic way by using creative advisors to evaluate the songs and productions at various stages, from the presentation of the original song to its shaping and evolution, to its recording and release.

Indeed, the Monkees' follow-up single, "I'm a Believer" (November 1966), reveals even more about the band's distinctive place in the LA pop music industry. This song came from another up-and-coming talented songwriter, Neil Diamond, signed to Screen Gems. Diamond had already released his own material as a recording artist but continued to write songs for others. While "I'm a Believer" remains a distinctive pop gem on its own, a certifiable classic, these back-to-back hits betray the system behind the Monkees project. Few bands retained access to this kind of catalog, a veritable jukebox of potential songs.

Kirshner put the gears in motion. He recognized the potential of "I'm a Believer" as soon as he heard it from Diamond, and then commissioned a recording session in New York, overseen by Jeff Barry, Diamond's producer.

Can you imagine a more perfect pop song than "I'm a Believer?" Clearly, few people could in the 1960s as it became one of the decade's biggest charters, fixed at the top spot for almost two months. When Top 40 stations added up the numbers for the whole decade, "Believer" floated from station to station across the nation in various positions in the Top 5 stratosphere, a tremendous achievement considering its neighbors: the Supremes, the Beatles, the Rolling Stones. Along with "Clarksville" and "Believer," the Monkees' fans hold songs like "Daydream Believer," "Pleasant Valley Sunday," and "For Pete's Sake" close to their hearts, but no other song from the group dominated the charts or endured thereafter as strongly as "I'm a Believer." Diamond, the studio musicians, and Jeff Barry's production deserve much of the credit, as does the vocal performance by Dolenz.

Though recorded in a New York studio, "I'm a Believer" echoes the California sound from the start. It slips in with a catchy three-chord whistling organ riff and a twangy guitar straight out of a classic surf-rock number. Before you know it, the big breathy acoustic guitar and vocals slip in on the final beat of the intro, kick-starting the song into its snappy beat. A full guitar strum ushers in the first verse, pushed forward in the mix, with a bass-heavy depth giving the guitar a rich presence. Precisely layered in the mix with technical rigor, the fullness of the sound of the guitar generates an acoustic intimacy, as if the guitar player was in your presence, accentuating the simple chords of the tune. Like the best pop, it invites the listener into the experience, as if you too could play along with the song, or at the very least clap along. The engineering in this way, on top of the inventive arrangement of the triadic chord structure, adds to the song's carefree breezy vibe.

Dolenz delivers the verses with just the right resignation and wistful breathiness to match the song's theme. He, and the engineers, take full advantage of the recording process, exploiting the microphone to sing softly and capture his dramatic breathing. Moreover, Dolenz sings the first verse within a narrow range, an acquiescence to the initial verses and their emotional uncertainty, consciously holding back his full, and quite powerful, vocal range. In the cadence leading up to the chorus, Dolenz most effectively and dramatically employs his engineered proximity to the microphone, as he precedes the defeated lines with full breaths before his slow-exhale delivery, a vocal parallel to the descending scale of the chords, until he pitches up subtly on the final word "dreams" (as do the chords). All through this cadence, Dolenz artfully releases his lines and his breathing now with a tinge of euphoria, even adding an "Ahhhh" of satisfaction. Then he unleashes on the release of the chorus, exuberantly throttling the lines, almost wailing.

In his ridiculously stiff yet earnest attempt to understand (and show off his appreciation of) rock and pop, Leonard Bernstein, then conductor for the New York Philharmonic, plucked "I'm a Believer" from the air as one of the few songs he chose to analyze directly on his softcore-radical-chic 1967 TV special *Inside Pop: The Rock Revolution*, a self-declared effort by grown-ups to understand youth and their music. Sitting at the piano like a schoolmaster, the silver-maned Bernstein headbangs along with some pop songs, sings a few selections in a flatly tonal voice, all the while admiring their inventive spirit (unsurprisingly, the Beatles command a lot of his attention). From a few Beatles tunes to the Left Banke's "Pretty Ballerina," he skips quickly to "I'm a Believer":

> Even so commonplace a number as the Monkees' recent hit "I'm a Believer" has one noteworthy musical twist. It's going along in the standard gospel shouting tradition [and here Bernstein sings the chorus accompanying himself on piano] and now suddenly here's the cadence
>
> [Bernstein performs it, ending on the D chord.]
> What a place to end on!
> [He plays the D chord again.]
> Totally unexpected chord!

The surprise comes from the use of the F# accidental in the cadence, especially if Bernstein heard the song rooted in G Mixolydian, in which case the progression would follow C, G, F, or D Minor, and thus the D Major chord is "totally unexpected." Bernstein likely found it surprising because the song is written in G Mixolydian and the F sharp changes the modality strongly to G Ionian or G Major. It's the only "clue" that the song is rooted in G Major. Diamond's melodic sensibility intuited a return to the next verse by using the D Major (V) to cadence back to G Major. Landing on a C Major triad or a D minor triad—the correct Mixolydian moves—didn't jive with the pop gospel sound. And that tricky mix tickled Bernstein's ears.

Then Bernstein imagines a rhetorical response to his surprise: "Well, what's so great about that chord? It's ordinary. We've had much more sophisticated and adventurous harmonies in pop music of the thirties. What about Gershwin? What about Duke Ellington? 'Sophisticated Lady,' with those rich chromatic parallel seventh chords." And then, from the D chord's snappy twist in "I'm a Believer," Bernstein launches into an acute analysis of the subtext of pop music—its rejection of certain musical traditions (roll over Beethoven)—and its limited but robust aesthetic parameters:

> That's the whole point. This pop generation has rejected that old chromatic sound as too sophisticated. The sound of an older, slicker generation. The old-fashioned sound of the cocktail lounge. This new music is much more primitive in its harmonic language. It relies more on the simple triads. The basic harmony of folk music . . . Within [pop's] restricted language, all these new adventures are simply extraordinary.[2]

All that from a simple chord in "I'm a Believer."

And more, for within the parameters spelled out by Bernstein, "I'm a Believer" perfectly exemplifies pop's attributes. Its chord structure works within the harmonic language of the folk tradition. Built mostly around three chords with the Mixolydian mode popping in—a little twist that always worked in pop—the song could easily fit into a "folk and roll" recording by the Everly Brothers, Jan and Dean, or Sonny and Cher (any of these artists would have made it a hit). An upbeat rhythm in 4/4 time, it taps into the gospel tradition underlying so much of pop. Though Bernstein passes rather quickly over the song's links to this tradition, his analysis accords with a more recent musicologist's recognition of this connection. Thomas Brothers hears gospel patterns over a hundred years old in pop and rock, what he unearths as the "ring shout" tradition in nineteenth-century African American churches: straining vocals to indicate authentic emotion, clapping and rhythmic movement to signify communal harmony. These elements, he argues, remain alive in popular music today.[3] Neil Diamond mastered the form.

Bernstein appreciates elements like the surprising D chord closing out the cadence to the chorus of "I'm a Believer" as real inventions in terms of pop's "basic English (so to speak)," not just as tricks or show-off devices. Pop's aesthetic parameters pushed its practitioners to twist around the form within its boundaries: triadic harmonics, a verse-chorus-verse structure, the hook and foregrounding of melodic lines, among other formal elements. Neil Diamond understood these principles, absorbing them through pop artists like Buddy Holly, the Everly Brothers, and Ritchie Valens, even as he reached back to the form's gospel roots. The whole school of composers at Screen Gems appreciated the aesthetic principles underscoring pop and rock compositions. They understood what Bernstein meant in his sermon to the TV audience without needing to hear any lecture. That understanding unified these artists; then their management, working with the same principles, scoured their work to match it with artists like the Monkees.

Always tuned into new developments, Boyce and Hart chiseled "(I'm Not Your) Steppin' Stone," the flip side to "I'm a Believer," in the style of the thumping garage rock quaking through the West Coast. "Stone" slams on its four-chord pattern, adding a skipping accent in a droning hypnotic call to dance. A swirling organ simmers through the slams, hiccups, and chord changes while the chorus chants, hums, and sings the first vowel to release the full statement with a final force. Again, Micky dramatically enacts the song in his lead vocals. He starts with a pent-up, gurgling whisper, each word clipped and tight, and then cuts loose to his wild yelling and singing.

By the midsection, the song breaks down, dropping out all the instruments save for the essential fuzzed-out bass. Rather than jumping to a middle-eight or instrumental solo, it simply and suddenly slams up the tempo with smashing chords and drums, a wild sped-up chorus, and backup vocals chanting the melody like a war cry. This break perfectly captures the joyful abandon—the anarchy—of garage rock: screw the middle-eight, it says, let's just repeat but faster! At any rate, the song demonstrates the work of dedicated songwriters picking up on trends and working with a style to generate an original work.

Another masterly production by Jeff Barry and his artist Neil Diamond, "A Little Bit Me, A Little Bit You," their third single (March 1967), picks up on the same clap and shout shuffle of "I'm a Believer" with a slightly mellower groove. Handclapping lays down the beat from the start with the big guitar strums ringing through the air just like in Diamond's previous hit for the Monkees. Barry mixed the handclaps upfront in the production, enhancing its communal vibe. Even when Davy starts singing and a tambourine (on the third measure) and bass join the electric clavinet and guitar, the claps remain crystal clear through the number, carrying the beat all the way. The guitarists—three of them for the session—lay down full strums in quarter notes and then two quick half notes, a skiffle effect echoing Diamond's heroes the Everly Brothers, especially hinting at the hopscotch strumming on their classic "Wake Up Little Susie."

The bass notes on the clavinet add drama to the big guitar strums and fill out the space on the third and fourth measures, a nice pairing of acoustic and electric sounds, effectively bringing its sonic dimension into the 1960s—in other words, a step forward from the song's otherwise strong roots in the already Golden Age pop of Buddy Holly or the Everlys. The clavinet had only been manufactured and released in the early 1960s (the Clavinet 1 debuted in 1964). It delivered a spacious yet tinny sound, echoing the ring of striking a piano key though the pitch sustained itself without fading. Some compared the sound to an electronic suturing of harpsichord and piano. But the big echo of the guitars gives the song its real distinction, and like "Believer," and much of Diamond's work at this time, adds to the communal vibe of the song, the sense that the listener can join in, sing, and clap along. Barry captures this intimacy by pushing the guitars up in the mix and enhancing their frontal effects with three guitars by the great New York session musicians Hugh McCracken, Al Gorgoni, and Don Thomas.

Jones takes the lead here, a savvy decision that brings out the breathy yearning and reassurance of the lyrics in his cool, hushed delivery. Berry and Jones exploit the microphone by moving close so that it captures his exhales as dramatic moments in the song, evoking intimacy. Jones offers up the verses in a soft, clipped diction, staying within a limited range, matching Diamond's clipped wordplay (words that start a line repeat at the line's end). Moreover, the verses address the conflicts of the couple in exposition so Jones's relatively affectless delivery reserves its emotional release for the more dramatic bridge. Here, as Jones expresses his desires in the lyrics, he stretches out words and vowels in his breathy releases, raising and lowering his pitch, especially as he reaches the song's chorus.

The 45's flipside reveals Michael Nesmith as a keen and developing student of pop songwriting. His early work as a songwriter mostly operated in the style of folk, with a studied eye on Dylan, according to Nesmith's own accounting, and a touch of country coming through. He honed his approach to flavor the folk with lyrics bending more towards pop so that a publishing company bought the rights to his work and landed him a few records. Working with the Monkees, Nesmith understood the need to produce more rock- and pop-inflected numbers, and this flipside, "The Girl I Knew Somewhere," revealed his studies.

The song kicks in with some muted flicks on an electric guitar's chords, with full strums punctuated by palming the strings to hold back their resonance, a creative twist on the similar effects of volume control on Harrison's "I Need You," which the chord changes here echo. But the song clocks in at a faster beat, swinging into motion with McCartneyesque bass-fingering twirls (played by Chip Douglas). Dolenz then urgently rushes through the words up high in his vocal range without a discernable breath, until he drops down in pitch for the final line of each verse. Peter Tork—indeed all the Monkees play on this track for the first time on a recording—cuts in with a chirpy, hyper harpsichord solo, and pop-baroque embellishments after the title lines.

The haunting lyrics offer a complex variation on a love song featuring a spurned lover, somehow reminded of a previous betrayal or broken romance, and so paranoid that he fails to trust a new lover. The rhyming scheme parallels the fragmented emotions, such that the rhymes occur on words within the middle of sentences, their logic tailing off on the syntactical completion, splitting the rhymes up here and there, at least for the first verses. The lyrics tumble over each other (Nesmith's verses often seem like the wordy ramblings of an auctioneer) as the verse sustains a single chord for four measures and drops down to the chord's roots as he defeatedly recalls his former lover. The triadic chord structure derived from the same traditions Nesmith explored in his early folk period, only he adapted it effectively to the pop format here, particularly with the revved-up beat. It slyly slips into a minor chord to dip into the bridge and plays around with suspended chords, winking at Nesmith's folk roots and the British Invasion at the same time. The Monkees' management team made the right choice: "A Little Bit Me, A Little Bit You" hit No. 2 and topped playlists all over; Nesmith's nifty number climbed to No. 39 on the *Billboard* chart, an impressive feat.

Boyce and Hart expanded on their contributions to the hit singles with other tunes, trying out songs for potential singles or building up material to fill out albums. "Gonna Buy Me a Dog" purchased much of its humor on the by now hokey chord structure and foot-stomping, knee-slapping rhythm of its delivery. The hokey-jokey lyrics draw on the simple slaphappy singsong of the strumming and drumming and perfectly predictable playing out of its chord changes, so that the old-fashioned accompaniment echoes the silly simplicity of the lyrics. Part of the jokiness buys into the fact that rock and pop had moved on in subtle or striking ways from such down-home formal mechanics. The performance—from the lyrics to the backup musicians—mocks rootsiness as part of the overall comedy. Elvis Presley camped it up again and again in rock's foundational era on songs like "Hound Dog," a performance that amounted to a sonic striptease act but did so almost ten years earlier, so the humor on this song, still effective, already seemed past its expiration date. The laughter, bantering quips, and corny sound effects buy more humor in case listeners shortchanged the silly lyrics and delivery.

"Tomorrow's Gonna Be Another Day," a song Boyce wrote with Steve Venet, works in the same chord pattern, and basically the same rhythm, as "Gonna Buy Me a Dog." Management picked both to fill out the albums rather than 45s or even B-sides, an easy decision in 1966 when the airwaves offered listeners fuzzed-out burners like "96 Tears" or the Kinks deploying power chords to propel the beat on songs (rather than the beat backing up old blues chord progressions). Even "Last Train," which operated in the same triadic pattern, pumped along with more variation, driving the first few verses through a sustained chord, and then dropping down to the 4th. Arranging songs in such deviations on the three chord patterns of pop remained the distinctive challenge for songwriters. Still, the repetition of the title in different stanzas breaks up some of the predictability, and the "Hey Hey Hey Hey" chirps perk up the song, with the slide guitar spicing up the mix. The song would hold up on any Stones album.

What can we say about "(Theme from) The Monkees?" The less the better, according to most of the Monkees themselves. Never released as a single, it still charted on Top 40 stations across the nation, revealing the systemic power of tying the music to the TV show. What other band recorded a theme song about themselves, as the embarrassed Monkees asked again and again? Still, this song written to order—the TV show's producers insisted on a title sequence song—reveals the strengths of Boyce and Hart as a songwriting team. In this case, they understood that the Monkees project modelled itself on the Beatles, but they expanded that model to include broader British Invasion tropes and sounds like the Dave Clark Five, the Kinks, and the Who, and injected these influences into this song. The Who cut a number very close to a declaratory theme song in "My Generation," and Boyce and Hart evoke similar themes here—talking about their generation—as well as power chords reverberating through full measures. They even include a wild discordant break in the middle, admittedly shorter and softer than the rave-up in the Who's song. The full measure strums, finger snapping, and whispered verses build directly on the Dave Clark Five's "Catch Us If You Can" (itself a title song for their own Beatlesque film), along with the machine gun snare fills that ripple through both songs.

All this time, in the same vein, staff writers Goffin and King looked at their neighbors on the charts, new arrivals like the Beatles, the Rolling Stones, and Bob Dylan, and noted the changing structures of their medium, the move away from straightforward love songs to ones laced with social commentary, stinging satire, and ennui: "Mother's Little Helper," "Subterranean Homesick Blues," or "Nowhere Man." These songs expanded the range of pop themes by tackling more complex, challenging material, and wedding them to the appealing form of pop and rock. Goffin pushed his writing partner to move in this direction, constructing 1967's Beatlesque "Pleasant Valley Sunday" exactly within this framework.

Goffin paints his satirical survey of the suburbs through a series of characters: a rock group, a neighbor mowing their lawn, Mrs. Gray, and Mr. Green (nods to the characters inhabiting landscapes like "Penny Lane," "Eleanor Rigby," or Dylan's "Mr. Jones"). Pride over well-manicured roses and lawns paints a picture of sterility, like a sonic version of the suburban setting of that year's *The Graduate*. The houses all look the same, television sets dominate the interiors, and the narrator remains numb, losing touch with his own soul, longing to escape somewhere (perhaps like the kids learning how to play the song). In identifying the suburbs as a land of status symbols, any subtlety slips away. Still, the song registers the new directions Goffin found so compelling in Dylan and others. Its sheer energy and the performances excuse the dated if still effective lyrics.

Chip Douglas, the producer of the Monkees' version, took King's slower, looser demo of the song and injected it with an edgier, faster sound, more in keeping with the spirit of those who inspired Goffin to begin with. Mike Nesmith recalls Douglas claiming, "We need a riff like in 'Paperback Writer,' 'Last Train to Clarksville,' 'Day Tripper.' How does this riff sound? He played the riff to 'Pleasant Valley Sunday.'"[4] At any rate, the anecdote offers yet another example of elements of the system coming together, here a producer understanding how a riff would enhance the work of the two songwriters.

Boyce and Hart captured the primal drive of garage rock in "She" and "Valleri," two numbers they wrote while punching the clock for the Monkees project. Recorded in August 1966, "She" kickstarts its mesmerizing skip-beat rhythm with an echo of "Louie Louie," hops and jumps through its herky-jerky power chords like "Wild Thing," and its exploding cadence out of the middle-eight rides like the build on "It's My Life." It holds its own with all these sources of inspiration. Winding through the erratic slams of guitar full strums, Bobby Hart's hypnotic organ slinks and twirls like a sonic snake charmer, a musical metonymy matching the song's theme: the mesmerizing allure of "She." With its vocals running from blaring yowls to breathy releases, the song is perfectly pitched to Micky's prowess as a rock singer. Some of the song's edge comes from the harmonies that remain just a little off. The Candy Store Prophets back it up with perfect grind and sharp staccato timing, injecting it with just the right balance of ragged rock and snappy synchronized rhythm.

Boyce and Hart picked up the same strains on "Valleri," adding fuzz guitar; the RCA engineer was familiar with the form, having worked on the Stones' "(I Can't Get No) Satisfaction" sessions, to which this song's lick owes more than a little debt. The song skitters and stomps through its brassy chords, synthesizing garage rock and classic 1950s hop-skip beats. The title was made to an order from Kirshner to deliver a song with a titular girl's name, and while the melismatic chorus whines out "Valleri," Louie Shelton adds a brilliant flamenco guitar riff to two different parts of the song, an acknowledgment of the eclectic sampling employed by pop songs (the sitar opened the door for this practice). The simplicity of the pop song form invited novelty, and a minor variation could add a distinction: a sitar, a fuzz guitar, a flute, or French horn solo. Shelton's flamenco guitar solo works in the same vein, adding an enticing twist to an otherwise great rocker.

Boyce and Hart's "Words" takes them in a groovy, jazzy, moody direction, with echoes of the Zombies. Tork's delayed lyrical responses (and their reverb) to Micky's leading lines add a spellbinding sonic space to the song, like some dreamy commentary on the preceding lines. Chip Douglas's basslines kick the recording to another level, driving its explosive buildup and bringing it back down to its jazzy groove. The song also allows Dolenz to exercise his vocal variation again, moving from breathy expressions on the verses to a wild pitch on the bridge and chorus.

"Valleri" and "Words," among other songs, demonstrate the reach of Boyce and Hart in creating the sound of the Monkees: the Los Angeles vibe of combining elements of folk and rock, the Beatles and the British Invasion, and the garage rock sound that simplified elements of these influences: clangy, twangy fuzz, with upfront barre chords and foregrounded beat. That depth and reach come out in the fact that final releases of these songs, first laid down in the studio in 1966, came out as late as '67 and '68. Reaching back to these songs when looking for new material in the relatively later part of the band's career, the Monkees and their managers confirmed the formative role Boyce and Hart played in shaping their sound.

Peter Tork and Micky Dolenz even got in on a little songwriting, inspired by the group's success and learning on the job. Tork worked on "For Pete's Sake" with Joey Richards, which lays down a groovy guitar lick and breezy easy lyrics skimming the surface of the summer-of-love images. Tork plays a C7 grip, just the inner four strings, and takes it up a whole two frets, the top string becoming the ninth of the chord, the simmering syncopated guitar licks lending the song a jazzy breeze. Dolenz played with similar tropes in "Randy Scouse Git," riffing on his visit to London, gripes about long hair, the stately Beatles, and a saucy title. An energetic chorus jumpstarts some real rock ravings from Dolenz accompanied and accentuated by rollicking, banging timpani. In the end, the Monkees themselves added only about twenty songs to their records. As late as 1969, they still drew most of their songs from the Screen Gems stable of writers, and even then often from the 1966–7 recordings.

The unique facet of the Monkees project involved streamlining the usual process of publishing a song and then finding a performer to gamble on its release as a recording. This streamlining process remained particularly distinctive in this mid-1960s period since most of the major performers wrote their own material at this time. True, the pop charts still included performers who drew on the system of songwriters working with publishers and with producers ("A&R men") to connect them with appropriate material. But the Monkees presented themselves in the TV show, publicity campaigns, journalism, and their fundamental model—the Beatles but also the Stones or the Dave Clark Five—as a band performing (albeit, mostly miming) their own material. Almost everyone knew—from articles on their auditions, to features on their backup band and songwriters and producers, to the standard identification of songwriters on their record labels—this wasn't really the case.

In this case, the songwriters, the performers, and the recordings were housed under the same roof as Screen Gems-Columbia Music, the publisher. The revenue streams flowed from one branch to the other. Aldon's original contracts with its songwriters promised that Kirshner's company would fulfill its role—its *raison d'être*—of matching songs with artists to deliver hits on the recorded versions and therefore bringing in revenue (split between the publisher and writer or writers). More than good faith applied since the shared revenue, in fact, ensured that the publisher would do their best to land the song with a recording artist as that avenue offered the only revenue for the publisher. Before recordings became the main commodity of the music market, selling sheet music was the primary job of the "publisher": hence, the name.

Ordinarily, before a performer recorded a song, the record company obtained a license from the publisher granting permission (generally granted as it offered potential revenue). With the Monkees, of course, this entailed only a lateral move. The royalty rate remained the same as any standard license: 2 cents to the publisher for every record sold. In the case of the Monkees—and not an uncommon case, in this regard—the publisher's royalties exceeded those of the Monkees for the record sales, at least on the first four albums and first few singles. With no strong bargaining position to leverage, the Monkees received a low royalty rate of 1.25 percent per album.[5] The Monkees, of course, gambled—correctly in this case—on the lower rate (2 to 3 percent represented the norm for new bands, with proven artists demanding much higher percentages),[6] knowing that the project would likely generate far more sales than a typical debut album given the synergy of the parent companies: the NBC television series and the record promotion and distribution by RCA Victor.

The stable of songwriters at Screen Gems kept their royalty streams open beyond those coming solely from the Monkees' productions. A glance at the *Cashbox* record charts in May 1967 puts *More of the Monkees* at the top, containing two Boyce and Hart compositions. But the songwriting team also pulled in royalties from songs on albums like Andy Williams's *Born Free*—at No. 11—Paul Revere and the Raiders' *Greatest Hits*—at No. 12—Ed Ames's *My Cup Runneth Over*—at No. 15—Herman's Hermits' *There's a Kind of Hush All Over the World*—at No. 22—while the first Monkees album was still hanging around at No. 23. We could perform a similar analysis with Goffin

Boyce and Hart spread their bets, and revenue streams, beyond the Monkees.

and King or Neil Diamond and the many ways they spread their bets and fortunes across other acts beyond the Monkees. In the cases of Diamond, and Boyce and Hart, the composers also pursued their own careers as performers. Driving all these endeavors was the pursuit of royalties from their copyrights on the songs.

When the Monkees' handlers initially rang out for material from Kirshner's team of writers, most of his East Coast talent fell silent, sniffing at the synthetic band. The band's instant success changed their tune so that the second album suddenly featured contributions from no fewer than twelve different writers. Monkeemania may not have impressed them as much as a mania for money. On top of the royalties collected from sales came those flowing from public performances of their songs, a revenue stream collected by BMI or ASCAP, and one form of fuel (besides the love of creation) in the drive for a hit. Boyce's 1967 quarterly BMI logging statement accounts for the power of performance royalties, the incentivizing drive they offer to the writers. BMI compiled these lists for songsmiths (and their publishers), surveyed radio stations, checked the logs of playlists maintained by most radio stations, collated these with other performances (television, film, live gigs), and collected the money owed, funneling it to the writers and their publishers.

For the quarter ending September 30, 1967, Boyce still earned royalties on "Come a Little Bit Closer" (a 1964 hit), and continued

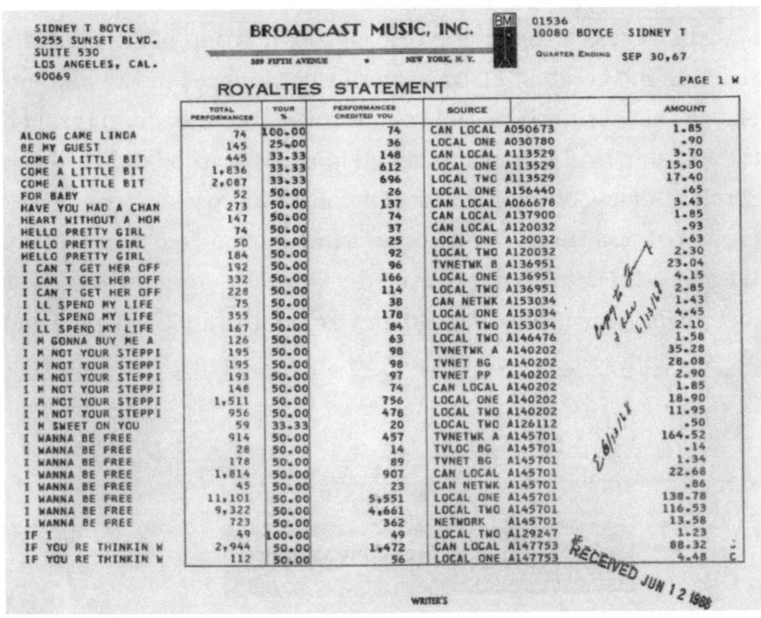

SIDNEY T BOYCE
9255 SUNSET BLVD.
SUITE 530
LOS ANGELES, CAL.
90069

BROADCAST MUSIC, INC. BMI
589 FIFTH AVENUE • NEW YORK, N. Y.

01536
10080 BOYCE SIDNEY T
QUARTER ENDING SEP 30,67

PAGE 1 W

ROYALTIES STATEMENT

	TOTAL PERFORMANCES	YOUR %	PERFORMANCES CREDITED YOU	SOURCE		AMOUNT
ALONG CAME LINDA	74	100.00	74	CAN LOCAL	A050673	1.85
BE MY GUEST	145	25.00	36	LOCAL ONE	A030780	.90
COME A LITTLE BIT	445	33.33	148	CAN LOCAL	A113529	3.70
COME A LITTLE BIT	1,836	33.33	612	LOCAL ONE	A113529	15.30
COME A LITTLE BIT	2,087	33.33	696	LOCAL TWO	A113529	17.40
FOR BABY	52	50.00	26	LOCAL ONE	A156440	.65
HAVE YOU HAD A CHAN	273	50.00	137	CAN LOCAL	A066678	3.43
HEART WITHOUT A HOM	147	50.00	74	CAN LOCAL	A137900	1.85
HELLO PRETTY GIRL	74	50.00	37	CAN LOCAL	A120032	.93
HELLO PRETTY GIRL	50	50.00	25	LOCAL ONE	A120032	.63
HELLO PRETTY GIRL	184	50.00	92	LOCAL TWO	A120032	2.30
I CAN T GET HER OFF	192	50.00	96	TVNETWK B	A136951	23.04
I CAN T GET HER OFF	332	50.00	166	LOCAL ONE	A136951	4.15
I CAN T GET HER OFF	228	50.00	114	LOCAL TWO	A136951	2.85
I LL SPEND MY LIFE	75	50.00	38	CAN NETWK	A153034	1.43
I LL SPEND MY LIFE	355	50.00	178	LOCAL ONE	A153034	4.45
I LL SPEND MY LIFE	167	50.00	84	LOCAL TWO	A153034	2.10
I M GONNA BUY ME A	126	50.00	63	LOCAL TWO	A146476	1.58
I M NOT YOUR STEPPI	195	50.00	98	TVNETWK A	A140202	35.28
I M NOT YOUR STEPPI	195	50.00	98	TVNET BG	A140202	28.08
I M NOT YOUR STEPPI	193	50.00	97	TVNET PP	A140202	2.90
I M NOT YOUR STEPPI	148	50.00	74	CAN LOCAL	A140202	1.85
I M NOT YOUR STEPPI	1,511	50.00	756	LOCAL ONE	A140202	18.90
I M NOT YOUR STEPPI	956	50.00	478	LOCAL TWO	A140202	11.95
I M SWEET ON YOU	59	33.33	20	LOCAL TWO	A126112	.50
I WANNA BE FREE	914	50.00	457	TVNETWK A	A145701	164.52
I WANNA BE FREE	28	50.00	14	TVLOC BG	A145701	.14
I WANNA BE FREE	178	50.00	89	TVNET BG	A145701	1.34
I WANNA BE FREE	1,814	50.00	907	CAN LOCAL	A145701	22.68
I WANNA BE FREE	45	50.00	23	CAN NETWK	A145701	.86
I WANNA BE FREE	11,101	50.00	5,551	LOCAL ONE	A145701	138.78
I WANNA BE FREE	9,322	50.00	4,661	LOCAL TWO	A145701	116.53
I WANNA BE FREE	723	50.00	362	NETWORK	A145701	13.58
IF I	49	100.00	49	LOCAL TWO	A129247	1.23
IF YOU RE THINKIN W	2,944	50.00	1,472	CAN LOCAL	A147753	88.32
IF YOU RE THINKIN W	112	50.00	56	LOCAL ONE	A147753	4.48

RECEIVED JUN 12 1968

WRITER'S

Monkees business and more: Boyce's royalty statements.

to rack in dough for "Steppin' Stone," "Last Train to Clarksville," "(Theme from) The Monkees," and "I Wanna Be Free." The last brought in royalties from several sources as it was covered by Andy Williams, Trini Williams, and Floyd Cramer as well as the Monkees. New royalty streams bubbled up with the Monkees' recent recordings of "She" and "Words," the former only appearing on the band's second album earlier that spring. Still, "She" lured in a lot of airplay as well as a performance on the TV show. "Words" sweet-talked its way onto the B-side of the band's single just at the end of the reporting period for BMI's quarterly accounting, but already generated some early royalty numbers for Boyce and Hart. In this case, "Words" tells us an open secret about the royalty process. A writer got the same royalty check for retail sales whether they made the A-side or B-side on a 45; of course, the A-side promised more radio play and therefore additional royalties, burnishing its appeal beyond the bragging rights of achieving an "A-side." But scoring the B-side promised equal retail returns on any 45 with an A-side hit.

The access to a catalog of songs by a group of songwriters remains the greatest distinction of the Monkees in the marketplace. That connection came about through the system, through the decision by Columbia to buy Aldon years earlier and establish Screen Gems-Columbia Music. Of course, the TV show helped to promote these songs. Yet no other band commanded such a team. If Boyce and Hart failed to deliver, the Monkees—or more precisely, their management team—could turn to Neil Diamond or Goffin and King. A mini song system within the larger system of the industry.

5

Air Guitar

The Monkees arrived at Chasen's Restaurant at 9039 Beverly Boulevard to put on a show. Chasen's, on the edge of Beverly Hills, served up a parental cocktail of cufflinked conversation, starched hair, and burnished squares, miles from Ben Frank's, the space and signifier that helped define the show's aesthetics. Dark in the daytime and night. Plush leather booths with wood-paneled frames. Little chandeliers with each bulb encased in a mini lampshade. More lampshades dotting the ensconced booths partitioning the dry-cleaned restaurant. For all this selective lighting, shadows loomed in and out of the space. A place to separate yourself from any scene. Actor by trade, governor by pay, Ronald Reagan commandeered his own booth on demand. Old Hollywood sat still in the air.

The Chasen's audience for the Monkees consisted of TV executives, congregated here in late June 1966, a bunch of local affiliates tied to NBC's prime-time programming, in which *The Monkees* TV show would makes its debut in September. Affiliates from local stations around the country worked by contract with the larger network—NBC, in this case—to carry their programs in key time slots (7:30 p.m. to 11 p.m. or so) that would lure in major commercial advertisers, a boost to the local stations if the scheduled primetime shows took off in the ratings. The management team gathered these representatives here to pump up the number of sign-ups by affiliates, most of whom generally bought into the programming offered to them, but still retained the right to reject some shows.

The TV show's head writers prepared a sketch for the boys, who would come in for a quick appearance and then shuffle out, a safe introduction—moreover, one with no musical performance (the management team knew the boys couldn't play together, if, in some cases, at all). Just before they entered the restaurant, the boys informed their handlers that they had scrapped their script.

That's how a stuffed peacock (NBC's mascot) ended up stopping traffic on Beverly Boulevard. The Monkees dragged it outside and preceded to play volleyball with it. Back inside, Micky cut the lights for the entire restaurant. When things settled down finally, after an introduction, the band launched into their own comedy act and promptly bombed on "stage."

Bert Schneider had opposed the whole appearance since, according to *TV Guide*'s reporting, "he figured it for a square scene and the affiliates wouldn't dig it anyway." The network overruled him. Schneider proved right. "The affiliates were already hostile and what was not needed was a bunch of smart-aleck kids," he confirmed. "On the way out I heard an affiliate say, 'That's *The Monkees*? Forget it.'"[1] Rejections or reactions of misapprehension from executive types ("squares") confirmed the central drive of the show: to appeal to the "Ben Frank's-types," the younger generation, the counterculture. The question remained as to how that would translate into television ratings for this part of the whole package of the Monkees project.

Only 160 affiliates picked up the program as opposed to the typical 200 for a network show.[2] That gave it something of a hurdle to surmount, in addition to broadening its appeal beyond the potential teen or preteen market. In this regard, it's no surprise that most stations aired it in the 7:30 timeslot, just before the allegedly more mature primetime programming kicked in. The TV show lasted two seasons. The system determined the successful part of the enterprise by letting the market make the decision: the music side won out.

Rafelson and Schneider budgeted the show strictly, insuring a profit from each episode sold to the network. They put the show's writers on a weekly salary to develop stories and keep the costs of individual scripts for episodes to a minimum. The Monkees themselves got $600 a week. Apropos of a band essentially created in a Hollywood laboratory, Raybert tested their cast selections by running them through a "psychogalvanometer." This bit of science fiction belonged to the newly established Audience Studies, Inc., an industry polling and testing service and a subsidiary of Screen Gems. For this task, and in line with their general services, the company screened the tests for an audience, gathered through their survey practices, at Preview House on Sunset, a four-hundred-seat theater. A panel in front of the seats of the audience members offered them buttons with "like" or "don't like" options.[3]

"Just how computerized can pop become?" the young rock writer Nik Cohn asked.[4] Very, apparently.

When the foursome and the TV show got the green light from their surveys and from their network deal, Screen Gems pitched the program, to both the industry and the public, as a zany, hip, modern Pop art creation. In their promotional material, the company pushed the show's association with New Wave films and promised that the show would reflect the new techniques:

> To complement the zany storylines, the series will adopt a number of the off-beat moviemaking techniques that helped make runaway hits of such unconventional feature films as *A Hard Day's Night*, *Cat Ballou*, *Dr. Strangelove*, *Tom Jones*, and *The Knack*. Nonsequitorial [*sic*] dialogue will be used. Characters may dress two different ways in one scene. There will be shock, flip and unmatched cuts. Some sequences will be speeded up; others slowed down. Overexposure and underlighting will be utilized to achieve a feeling of uninhibited realism.[5]

Here they've linked the show to cutting-edge cinematic techniques and tones as symbolic of change. The French New Wave film movement, and startling products of international art cinema in general, strongly influenced some key American filmmakers—Stanley Kubrick and Richard Lester stand out in the list of films above—and soon burst into a powerful American film movement and culture, the kind Rafelson and Schneider would join with productions like *Five Easy Pieces* and *Easy Rider*, and highlighted by films like *Bonnie and Clyde* or *The Graduate*. Of course, Richard Lester achieved just such a synthesis on *A Hard Day's Night*. Lester recognized that the youthful sense of energy and rebellion enacted by the Beatles struck a cinematic match with the rebellious, energetic formal experiments and techniques of Godard and Truffaut.

Since the New Wave began in France as a blanket term for a youth culture, before it became known as a film movement, the cinematic synthesis to youthful popular culture like the Beatles and pop music retained a kind of cultural genetic code. A series of articles appeared in 1957 in *L'Express* recognizing a shift in French culture in different arenas and institutions—from Françoise Sagan, the nineteen-year-old literary sensation dominating international best-seller lists with *Bonjour Tristesse*, to Yves St. Laurent's new fashion design, but also to things like "juvenile attitudes to a style of living, including wearing black leather jackets and riding noisy motor scooters around Paris."[6] The journal dubbed the phenomenon a "new wave," and the phrase stuck to the filmmakers.

Truffaut used a hand-held camera to capture the movement and fleeting quality of life in his youthful protagonist in *The 400 Blows*. A whip pan blurs the screen with a sudden jump cut transporting the character to another scene. A freeze-frame captures a moment of emotional ambiguity. Unconventional camerawork and editing matched the youthful energy of his protagonist and its theme of aimless rebellion, insolent youth fighting the conformity, dreary regulation of adult life and institutions, trapped in his school or in his apartment, then bursting out as the camera races to keep up with him.

The New Wave brought new subjects—mostly young characters—to the screen and did so with new techniques (significantly, the French filmmakers leading the charge themselves were young), suggesting that traditional cinematic conventions reflected out-of-date values and old standards. The New Wave offered up new forms of storytelling, cutting up scenes into visual vignettes with fragments of dialogue and music mixed in rather than theatrical staging. In some cases, these techniques were linked to films that dealt with new attitudes about sexual relations and relationships. The narratives were loose and episodic, capturing emotional or psychological atmospheres. The camera moved through mobile close-ups and reframing, giving the formal expression a resonant inventiveness and spontaneity. Likewise, the films pulled images from art, magazines, and comic books—*Mad* magazine turns up in Godard, *Zazie dans le métro*, and *A Hard Day's Night*—suggesting a modern, media-saturated world and a Pop art approach to other art forms. It bordered on amateurishness but suggested authenticity—using the camera like a paintbrush, personal and intimate—especially compared to slick, big-budget films.

Godard included interviews in his fiction films—the press conference in *Breathless*, the headshot confessions in *Masculin-Feminin*—echoed in the cocktail press party in *A Hard Day's Night*. Indeed, when commissioned to direct the first Beatles movie, Richard Lester appropriated the New Wave style as a fitting cinematic complement to the wit, innovation, and youthful energy of the band. Unlike the Elvis Presley films, the Beatles played scripted versions of themselves, letting the film paint their personalities. The legendary film critic Andrew Sarris famously referred to it as "the *Citizen Kane* of jukebox movies." Seeing it, of course, spurred Rafelson and Schneider to develop the Monkees.

Raybert hired Larry Tucker and Paul Mazursky to develop the pilot script and set the model for the program. Upcoming TV writers, they were also young cinephiles mesmerized by the new art cinema tearing up old traditions of formal style, probing new subjects and breaking taboos on both ends. Like Rafelson, Mazursky would go on to write and direct films of the new Hollywood with his own homages to Fellini and the French New Wave. They took the job as a manifesto, surely encouraged to experiment by the producers, and finished their pilot script in August 1965.

THE MONKEYS

This script is not a conventional TV pilot. It should not be read as one, performed as one, or photographed as one.

Five years ago the terms "New Wave", "Cinema Verité", "Shock Cut", etc. were all experimental approaches to a new film style. Today, these same techniques are the conventions of modern film-making. People are lining up to see them in "Hard Day's Night", "Help", "The Knack", "Dr. Strangelove", "Tom Jones", "Cat Ballou", etc. They aren't new to movies anymore. But they are to television.

"The Monkeys" is a show conceived by and for young people. If you saw "Hard Day's Night" and said "hey, what's it all about anyway"...the picture was not made for you. But, if you are one of the countless millions* who dug the freshness, the exuberance, the charm of "Hard Day's Night"...then you're ready for "The Monkeys".

Yes. There is non-sequitorial dialogue. There are shock, flip, match and unmatching cuts. People dress two different ways in one scene. Music carries under a scene that was begun in an earlier scene. Film is speeded up, slowed down, over-exposed, under-lit.

Rules of film-making have changed. Today, film is pliable -- not some holy parchment demanding cautious treatment.

Read "The Monkeys" and...please...try not to compare it to the "Donna Reed Show". It's seven years later. Television is ready for the change. My mother is ready for the change. Are you ready for my mother? (Don't call her -- she's waiting in your outer office.)

*Note: Actually these millions are countable. Results of our survey (there are three staff members in mobile trucks now) will be in shortly. Until then -- "countless millions".

The first page of the pilot script offered a manifesto tying the show to youth and New Wave filmmaking.

The first page reads like a declaration of war: "This script is not a conventional TV pilot. It should not be read as one, performed as one, or photographed as one." It continues with a mini history lesson, mentioning recent films that shattered cinematic traditions and conventions (clearly the source for NBC and Screen Gems' promotional pamphlet):

> Five years ago the terms "New Wave," "Cinema Verité," "Shock Cut," etc. were all experimental approaches to a new film style. Today, these same techniques are the conventions of modern film-making. People are lining up to see them in "Hard Day's Night," "Help," "The Knack," "Dr. Strangelove," "Tom Jones," "Cat Ballou," etc. They aren't new to movies anymore. But they are to television.

New Wave. Cinéma vérité. Shock Cut. The writers evoke these concepts as catch-all descriptions of new experiments in filmmaking techniques. Shock cut likely refers to the staccato editing in Godard's films and its migration to Richard Lester's work with the Beatles in *A Hard Day's Night*, *Help!* or *The Knack . . . and How to Get It*. Cinéma vérité refers less to documentary form and more likely to the handheld cameras and the liberated movements of new forms of staging that suggested a spontaneity in these new films.

Their manifesto recognizes the tone and experimental style of the New Wave for its connections to youth:

> "The Monkeys" is a show conceived by and for young people. If you saw "Hard Day's Night" and said "hey, what's it all about anyway" . . . the picture was not made for you. But, if you are one of the countless millions who dug the freshness, the exuberance, the charm of "Hard Day's Night" . . . then you're ready for "The Monkeys."

Finally, they declare: "Rules of filmmaking have changed. Today, film is pliable—not some holy parchment demanding cautious treatment." Its pretentiousness is saved by its youthful exuberance and the energy of its call for experimentation and transformation. Interestingly, François Truffaut and Tony Richardson, leading filmmakers of these new waves, both wrote their own versions of manifestos and tied their respective calls for revolutionizing cinema to youth and to a generational shift. Mazursky likely didn't know that specifically, but he and his cowriter clearly picked up on the youthful rebellious energy with these films.

The show exercised these qualities by employing jump cuts, sped-up frame rates, slow motion, handheld camera, title-cards, and actors directly addressing the camera. Most of these techniques accompany slapstick sequences of the boys grappling with some comedically challenging situation or a straight-up chase, all of which still clearly reference *A Hard Day's Night* and the new cinema.

While New Wave films or *A Hard Day's Night* took on youthful topics, relationships, and even sexuality, the TV show mostly if not entirely avoided such themes. It usually set up a situation—a character seeks a job or gets a new job—and then let it play out for humor (like *Get Smart* or *Gilligan's Island*), just like other situation comedies. It also featured many actors in guest parts who made the rounds of the sitcom dial. The scripts rarely dealt with the band itself. Instead, they took plotlines—albeit ridiculously arch plotlines—that would work with a few twists on any number of shows: the band members get involved in a toy company whose management shifts to a computer; they get mistaken through circumstantial confusion as part of a spy ring; one of them gets a job; one of them falls in love, and so forth.

Several episodes ended with mock press conferences where the Monkees provide spontaneous answers to unscripted questions as themselves, a clear pastiche of the witty, clever, and zany press conferences the Beatles engaged in. You can see the real thing in a film like the Maysles brothers' *What's Happening! The Beatles in the* U.S.A. or their patter on TV shows, replicated in the New Wave-style press party in *A Hard Day's Night*: jumpy staccato editing undercutting the zippy one-liners. In the case of the Monkees, these interviews were performed on a sound stage with props and equipment in the background or on one of the outdoor sets on the studio lot. Like their screen tests, each Monkee proved quick on their feet or capable of thoughtful personal responses.

The TV show staged the band in a shared living space à la the Beatles' abode in *Help!*, though the Monkee mini-manor pales in comparison to the Liverpudlians' dynamic Pop art pad, with its color-coded living sections (the Dave Clark Five also share a pad in their flick *Catch Us If You Can*). Tucker and Mazursky's template script made it clear that the band's pad popped out with Pop art:

> INT. THE MONKEY'S PAD – DAY
> It is a large, one room house. The room is a reflection of the characters of the four boys. There are Pop Art posters on one wall, a large photo of Jeanne Moreau on another wall; a collage of newspaper items from various papers, every item about an incident at a zoo involving monkeys.[7]

The writing was on the wall in this first script: Pop art and Jeanne Moreau, the iconic French New Wave star.

On the actual program, the Monkees' funky bungalow features an assortment of props meant to signify on different levels: youthful bohemian bric-a-brac, a beach pad, and a zany Pop art commentary on domestic space. The seemingly random props likely sought to evoke the camp aesthetic of the times, with old movie posters, ventriloquist dummies, traffic signs, and quirky knick-knacks. The decor almost evokes the domestic trappings represented in Richard Hamilton's definitive Pop art masterpiece, *Just What Is It That Makes Today's Homes So Different, So Appealing?* (1956), with its collage of advertising products and cut-outs (comic book covers, TV sets, vacuums from ads, striptease and beefcake figures) forming its own mishmash of mid-century modern and older consumer goods. But the set here seems less calculated and thoughtfully arranged than any camp statement or Pop art construction like Hamilton's; the randomness more likely reflects the threadbare budget decisions, with a weak nod to the camp and bohemian spirit of the times.

The press consistently compared the show to the contemporary *Batman* TV series for its campy tone and target television audience: teens who could consume it through the lens of camp and preteens with only a vague awareness of the tone. KRLA *Beat*, for example, called it "a cross between *Batman* and *Help!*" In fact, looking back at this period, Batman seems like the secret connection between the new pop and rock, New Wave techniques, and Pop art. Adam West, with knowing eyes and elegant snark slipping through his Batman mask, appeared on the February 5, 1966 cover of KRLA *Beat* and called himself "the Greatest Put-on." Warhol and other Pop artists painted Batman on canvases (and Warhol posed as Batman's sidekick Robin (with his protégé Nico in Caped Crusader gear) for a magazine photo shoot). The Who covered the *Batman* TV theme song on their 1966 EP *Ready Steady Who*. The Beatles threw in the choral declaration of "Taxman" (on the titular song) before the guitar solo in homage to the show's theme song. One episode of *The Monkees* TV show featured a superhero fight doubling down on the camp with "Whammo" and "Blammo" word balloons explicitly referencing *Batman*. Early episodes of the series featured a few experiments with word balloons, clearly modelled on the same TV–comic book aesthetic synthesis.

When the *Washington Post* ran an article on the show, it characterized the program as NBC's "secret weapon aimed at Batman . . . It's not a zap gun. It's not even a roadblock for ABC's Batmobile. What it is, is a new show concocted to woo the younger generation away from the dynamic duo."[8] The article, like many in the months leading

America's Largest Teen NEWSpaper

KRLA Edition

BEAT

Volume 1, Number 47 LOS ANGELES, CALIFORNIA 15 Cents February 5, 1966

Batman: 'I'm the World's Greatest Put-On' . . . Page 2

Almost everyone targeted the Monkees as an answer to the campy, "Put-on" spirit of the *Batman* TV show.

up to the debut of the show and the records, transparently laid out the entire operation as "a wholly manufactured singing group" who come off "as a combination of the Beatles, the Dead End Kids and the Marx Brothers." It recognized the scandal as well: "Critics will cry foul. Longhairs will demand, outraged, that they be removed from the air. But the kids will adore The Monkees." It then outlined the audition process and the fact that "unlike other rock'n'roll groups, the boys had never performed together before." Finally, it speculated wittily that the group was brought together "presumably by guys in white coats with nets." Richard Lester found none of this amusing. He complained to a British reporter that the series completely plagiarized his work with the Beatles.[9]

With its debut in September, *The Monkees* found a welcome, if not immediate, audience with new fans and with many critics. Most recognized the show for its novel approach to the TV medium. Surprisingly, Jack Gould, the influential critic at the *New York Times* who notoriously attacked TV appearances by both Elvis and the Beatles, praised the show. "At least," he wrote, the show "is not like every other situation item on the home screen." Yet his approval becomes less surprising when he explains part of its appeal: "They've played down the rock'n'roll angle to where it's not much more than an incidental sonata and instead have conducted their mop-haired charges through assorted antics suggestive of The Marx Brothers in adolescence." Thus, Gould valorized this show about a rock band precisely because it avoided the music: "The Monkees are to be welcomed for joining the pursuit of chuckles rather than orgiastic studio squeals," a stab at the screaming audiences accompanying the TV appearances of the Beatles.[10]

Gould's praise sounds like tone-deaf criticism for a show about a rock band. Yet his approval betrays a truth. Micky Dolenz recognized this same contradiction in the program. "Although ours was uniquely set in the environment of the sixties pop scene," Dolenz noted, "that had little to do with what the show was about."[11]

Instead, the plots consisted of Davy falling in love with a princess, any one of the Monkees getting a job, Mike running for mayor, or spending the night in a haunted house. Rooted in the hip scene of the Sunset Strip and the British Invasion, *The Monkees* TV episodes nonetheless worked around familiar sitcom formulas that would easily work when mixed with other TV comedies at the time. Despite Mazursky's manifesto trumpeting the show's distinction from other sitcoms, the plotlines played along familiar scenarios. On the program's debut episode, the Monkees rescued a princess from her evil uncle. A few episodes later they got mixed up in a spy ring; they got stranded in a ghost town and held prisoner by bank robbers; Davy gets suckered into boxing lessons; they all get duped into dancing lessons.

The Monkees themselves protested at some of these TV conventions. By the second season, for example, the producers agreed to get rid of the canned laughter piped in on the soundtrack, a convention of the era. The costumes expanded to include hippie

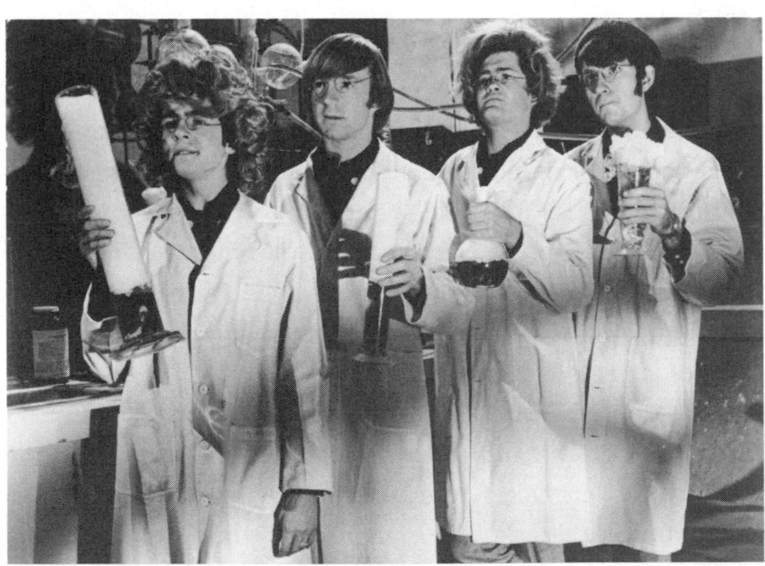

The TV comedy formula for a band mixed in a media lab: genre satire dominated the plotlines of *The Monkees*.

fashions. The boys successfully lobbied to get guest stars on the second season like Tim Buckley and Frank Zappa. Yet the plotlines continued. On the episode titled "The Monstrous Monkee Mash," for example, you guessed it: the Monkees encountered Count Batula, a Wolfman, a Mummy and a Frankenstein monster. Yes, in a spooky castle. More princesses and nefarious schemes too in Season Two.

A few episodes addressed the music scene, if only tangentially: grappling with a crooked music publisher, auditioning for a party or an event here and there. On "The Audition" (aka "Find the Monkees"), a television producer goes wild over a Monkees recording without knowing their name; he marshals a frenzied search to build a show around the unknown band, staging an audition as part of the process (no irony acknowledged). This episode uses this setup to mock high-concept band names and costumes: the Four Martians, the Four Agents, the Jolly Green Giants (all with matching costumes), a wink to the contemporary music scene (à la the Zombies or the Seeds), if by way of the Flintstones (the Beau Brummelstones, the Way-Outs).

That show also featured the longest post-episode interview scene with the boys on the topic of the recent clashes on the Sunset Strip. This Q&A allowed them to discuss the symbolic value of long hair as a meaningful style, the rights of free expression and its importance to youth. Long hair jokes and minor counterculture quips pop up here and there on various episodes, lacing the otherwise sitcom story lines with edible doses of generational winks. Overall, though, the show remained, as a Columbia ad promoting its syndication put it, "wholesomeness and family fun."

The Monkees inverted the relationship between television and authenticity. Television, in fact, represented a significant motif in the emerging rock mythology. It surfaced in stories about the dangerous allure of Elvis's sexuality, for example, with the now mythic story of cameras carefully tilted above his gyroscopic pelvis, its sensuous, sizzling shocks shakin' up TV's standards and practices. In this telling, television plays a villainous or withering role enhancing the authenticity of Presley's wild power and persona. Or take the tale of the Stones performing "Let's Spend the Night Together" on the *Ed Sullivan Show*. The fable goes that the stuffy host allegedly refused to let them perform the suggestive song, only to reach a compromise with the band: replacing the lyrics with "let's spend some time together." The band complied on air, but Jagger exaggerated an insolent eye roll on each delivery, prompting Sullivan to ban them from ever performing on the show again. They came back, of course, but that didn't ruin the story. Rock rebels yet again in this narrative, maintaining its authenticity in the face of this demanding and compromising medium. If television established any authenticity at this time, it was only through the medium's recording capacity: documentary, TV news, or reproducing dramatic literature (American Playhouse) won the highest praise from critics. Closer to home, in music culture, the liveness of a televised performance by Elvis or the Beatles retained true vitality. In these cases, television represented a conduit, a recording medium, faithfully transcribing an artistic performance that retains its own authenticity uncorrupted by the medium.

The Monkees flipped this equation—and never recovered from the "corruption"—in becoming a band fabricated *by* and *for* television. The medium *was* the message with the Monkees. Television didn't simply and neutrally deliver the band. The band, in some real sense, only existed because of television. But despite the McLuhanesque media vibes of the times, the medium of TV carried suspicions for its role in the system: the media-industrial complex and its attendant commercialism. Music needed to purify itself. Its industrial strength had grown, getting more complicated and larger. Any direct ties to television only confused or compromised rock's claims to authenticity.

Almost every major band performed on television, had "broken through" on television. But TV in these cases only served as a delivery platform, one among many—newspapers, magazines, radio, live concerts—if still the most important. Through this understanding or conception of the medium—of TV as recording medium—music and performers could reach millions, define themselves, promote themselves, harness the interstellar power of TV and still retain their authenticity. The key here is that their authenticity is supported through this definition of the medium. If merely appearing on television represented a form of corruption or compromise (as it would, perhaps, for certain other genres), Elvis or the Beatles would have been irrevocably tarnished.

In this sense, even rock purists accepted or tolerated certain aspects of the pop music industry (often seemingly begrudgingly). Tolerance or acceptance. Not acknowledgment. The Monkees concept foregrounded the system and the industrial aspects of modern music too strongly. The Beatles, Elvis, the Stones on Ed Sullivan, for rock purists, meant accepting the inevitability of aspects of the system so long as the artists sustained their own authentic identities. TV was a part of the game and, in the end, by defining it as a recording medium, it was then only a conduit, not a shaping force. But the Monkees took the medium itself as part of their identity or message. The quick cuts, the spatial and temporal jumps or disconnects in editing, the direct address and asides, the manipulation of frame rates, the anarchic pace and almost episodic digressions signified a New Wave attitude, an alliance with youth culture and young rebellion, all tied to the utopian and democratic energy of pop music, a link that signified the show's original inspiration (the energy of pop and the Beatles) and its commercial imperative.

With *A Hard Day's Night* and *Help!*, Richard Lester had fused New Wave cinematic techniques and youth culture. So a campy attitude towards acting, a slapstick, sped-up frame rate, or herky-jerky jump cuts would now signify a generational attitude and anarchic spirit as much as long hair or a wild polka-dot shirt or, indeed, a pop song. Rafelson and Schneider recognized the generational dimension

The Monkees miming a musical performance for a TV show sequence.

of these media tactics and brought them to television, the "cool" medium, imparting it with a contemporary topical signification, like Marshall McLuhan. Avoiding the television medium altogether, to some, could represent a square, old-fashioned refusal to recognize its modernity. Yet the emerging mythology of rock sought to distance the art form from the machinery of modern media, so that all the potential significance of televisual techniques were rendered empty signifiers. TV, public relations, and advertising, among other factors, were only accidentally or incidentally related to the centrality of the music, which defined—in very specific parameters—an artist's authenticity. By this measure, the Monkees failed the test.

Bam! Splatt! Kapow!

In fact, by the fall of 1966, the important value of authenticity in a band's persona pushed the management team to finally consider putting the band on the road in front of live audiences. Raybert realized a concert tour could enhance the Monkees' image as well as add another potential revenue stream to the overall enterprise. The delay in staging a tour probably related to the busy TV production schedule and testing the popularity of the project. Of course, the lack of experience on the part of half of the Monkees reinforced any initial hesitancy or even discussion of a real tour, especially when the production team heard the results of early rehearsals by the band. But tension developed with Michael Nesmith and Peter Tork and their desire to play a more prominent role in the musical recordings and perform as a genuine band.

Indeed, the first season's last episode seeks to address the open secret of the studio musicians. The episode is constructed as a documentary, breaking from the situation comedy format. It's essentially a staged documentary concert, set up entirely for the camera record, deliberately evoking the cinematic hysteria of Beatlemania. The imperative driving the episode comes out nakedly when Mike asks a young fan at a radio station what they would think if they knew the band didn't play their own instruments. "If you found out that none of us could play a note, couldn't carry a tune in a bucket, would you hate us?" he says on air. He's surprised when the fan says she wouldn't care. And when he asks why not, she says, "because you're putting people on pretty good," to the startled laughter of everyone. The proof was in the Put-on: no proof needed. Despite the fan pulling the rug out from under their feat, Mike persisted: "Okay, well for those skeptics out there who still don't believe that we play our own instruments, come down and tell 'em you know me and I'll get you in free."

A scene of fans clamoring behind a wire fence, excitedly awaiting the arrival of the Monkees, evokes now familiar images of Beatlemania. The microphone picks up chatter that a local radio station gave away the time and place of their arrival just that afternoon, no doubt to help the filmmakers stage the scene. One girl even asks the camera crew: "Is this the Monkees? I thought it was the Rolling Stones."

Close-ups of fans reacting as the Monkees deplane and scamper near the gates help to heighten the hysteria and leave the size of the crowd up to the audience's imagination. They artfully refuse to offer any wide shots so that we glean no sense of the size of the gathered crowd. From there, the episode cuts to the boys clowning around in a hotel room, taking in the local scenery with off-the-cuff wisecracks (Davy mocks the times with a "long-hair" joke about a horse and its mane), followed by crowds of a few dozen (mostly elementary school boys, oddly) here and there.

Finally, halfway through the half-hour episode we see the actual concert in front of a sizable audience. It documents the revue-style approach that the management set up for their tours. The Monkees play a handful of their songs on their own as a four-piece band. Then the individual Monkees perform essentially as solo artists with a back-up band of other musicians (most often, Boyce and Hart and their Candy Store Prophets), allowing Nesmith and Tork to demonstrate their musical skills. Peter plays a banjo on several songs. Nesmith performs some of his originals and some covers. Micky sings through his sketch, ending with a wild James Brown imitation, cape and all (on Ray Charles's "I Got a Woman"); Davy performs a few Broadway tunes. Then the four return to play as a band again, closing with a grungy version of "I'm Not Your Steppin' Stone," though for this episode the audio of the actual performance gets drowned out heavily by the screaming crowd.

Raybert recognized the need to legitimize the band through live musical performances, particularly since the musical side of this enterprise showed much earlier strength and potential long-term success than the television program. Under the agreement Screen Gems struck with Dick Clark Productions (a concert tour organization), the arenas got no more than a flat 10 percent of the gate, with Clark and Screen Gems splitting the remainder. They tested out the prospect with a concert in Hawaii, a strategic location far from most media attention. And not just any gig: they played at a local radio station's beauty contest and, thus, with a built-in audience. No need to sell tickets for their set of just over a dozen songs or so.

Then, in the summer of 1967, a real tour was organized of almost thirty dates between July and August from Florida up the East Coast through the Midwest and on to the Pacific Northwest, ending in Oregon and Washington. These concerts followed the revue format first seen on the TV concert: a few numbers performed by the Monkees as a quartet, then the individual members in solo spots backed up by the Candy Store Prophets, followed by a few more numbers by the quartet to close the show. Even when out front as a foursome, the Monkees were sometimes backed up by the Prophets.

The most frequent response to the concerts on the part of critics was surprise. Surprise that the Monkees could actually play musical instruments. Surprise that they could put on a good show.

Putting on a show: the Monkees proving they can play in a live concert.

"The Monkees didn't sound as full or polished as on their records," an Arizona critic noted of an early show, "but nonetheless dispelled any beliefs they are musically deficient."[12] Yet another motif surfaces almost as often: the sheer noise of the crowds and how that drowned out the music, sometimes casting some skepticism over the possibility of any discerning assessment of their real chops as musicians.

When it came to promotion of the Monkees' recordings, the TV show played the biggest role. From the start, the producers planned to feature two songs on every episode, a formula set from the beginning as one musical performance of a song and one song accompanying an action sequence (slapstick chases mostly, as in "Can't Buy Me Love" in *A Hard Day's Night*). In fact, an early internal company memo (from September 1965) reveals the formula as Screen Gems' Lester Sill requests two distinct pieces of music for the show from Don Kirshner: a theme song and another designated "The Chase." Nothing came of this request as Kirshner's East Coast office was unimpressed at this early stage of the show's development. Sill then got Boyce and Hart to compose music for the pilot. A few months later the pair had come up with the show's theme, two versions (slow and fast) of one of their previously composed songs—"I Wanna Be Free"—and a few other numbers. For the pilot, Boyce handled the lead vocals, backed up by the Candy Store Prophets crew. Once the show got picked up for network distribution, they rerecorded the vocals with various Monkees.

Still, the formula outlined in Sill's memo structured the music programming for every episode: a performance of a song and a song used as a soundtrack to a chase or slapstick frolicking. Added to this calculus was the timing of any newly released 45. "Last Train to Clarksville," for example, appeared in episodes two, three, and four, into early October, by which time it got designated a smash hit, reaching No. 1 a few weeks later. That pattern repeated itself with "I'm a Believer," "A Little Bit Me, A Little Bit You," "Daydream Believer," and so on. "Believer" played on successive episodes throughout December 1967, timed perfectly with its release that month as a 45. "A Little Bit" aired on the first season's penultimate episode in April, following its release in March. Flip sides and album cuts got airplay as well, frequently shooting these tracks to respectable numbers on the charts as a result.

The management team applied an exacting strategy to the use of music, replacing songs on reruns with timely new releases, and even shuffling songs around for promotion and simple exposure on the Saturday morning repeats. Reruns of the first season in 1967, for example, featured cuts from their newly released third album which replaced tracks from their first album when the earlier episodes debuted in 1966.

Consider this list of replacements to reruns of the first season in 1967, replete with newly released songs:

AIR DATE	NEW SONG ADDED	EPISODE TITLE
May 1, 1967	"A Little Bit Me, A Little Bit You"	Monkee See, Monkee Die
May 8, 1967	"You Told Me"	Royal Flush
May 15, 1967	"A Little Bit Me, A Little Bit You"	Your Friendly Neighborhood
May 22, 1967	"You Told Me"	Monkee vs. Machine
May 29, 1967	"Shades of Gray"	Success Story
June 19, 1967	"Randy Scouse Git"	The Spy Who Came in From the Cool
June 26, 1967	"For Pete's Sake"	I've Got a Little Song Here
July 10, 1967	"Words"	Here Come the Monkees (Pilot)
July 17, 1967	"Pleasant Valley Sunday"	The Case of the Missing Monkee
July 31, 1967	"Words"	Monkee Chow Mein
August 7, 1967	"Pleasant Valley Sunday"	Captain Crocodile
August 14, 1967	"Forget That Girl"	One Man Shy
August 21, 1967	"You Just May Be the One"	The Chaperone

All songs were culled from their recent album (*Headquarters*, released in late spring 1967) or their recent singles ("A Little Bit Me, A Little Bit You," "Pleasant Valley Sunday"). To drum up industry support and convince radio programmers of the "momentum" behind the new songs, the Monkees' team advertised this tactic to the trade press. "10 'HQ' Tunes in Monkees Rerun," for example, ran one *Billboard* article. "Ten songs from 'Headquarters,' the Monkees' latest album on Colgems," the article informed, "will be inserted into summer rerun episodes of their TV show."[13] Such transparency informed the band's engagement with their fans as they stirred up interest in the new album and the reruns in a letter to the fan club regarding *Headquarters*:

> You can help the Monkees by asking your favorite disc jockey and radio stations to feature songs from the album.
>
> Songs on the album will also be heard on The Monkees summer repeat television programs, so you can catch up on the episodes you missed, enjoy your favorite episodes again, and hear the new Monkees music all at once.[14]

You get a stronger sense of the success of the show in promoting the songs by considering album tracks on the charts. Certainly, DJs picked album tracks from many artists. But the timing of some of the Monkees' releases, particularly in the first season, sync up with their use on TV episodes. Even the theme song charted on many radio stations (Sill told the press at one point that they considered releasing it as a single). Likewise, "I Wanna Be Free" charted in the fall, after it accompanied a montage of Davy falling in love on a few early episodes.

All around the country, DJs often recorded songs off the TV show and aired them on their programs. The early 1968 single "Valleri" offers a case study of this kind of DJ support and in how the show added fuel to the promotion of the band's records. Two DJs in

Florida and another in Chicago allegedly taped the song from its first appearance on the TV show in early 1967 (for the record, Nesmith gamely mimes the brilliant flamenco-style guitar riff laid down by Louie Shelton on the recording). The song shot to the top of these station's playlists and requests. But as a potential vinyl 45 it sat on the shelf as the next batch of singles rolled out of the Monkees machine (understandably: "Pleasant Valley Sunday" and "Daydream Believer"). The rerecorded version of "Valleri" finally hit No. 3 on *Billboard*'s charts in early 1968.

In the very first season, news articles appeared steadily and consistently regarding the success of their records outpacing the television ratings. An article in *Record World* in March 1967 noted that "the TV show itself, while successful, had not been the phenomenon that the disks have been. Ratings have consistently put the show in the 20s and 30s."[15] But it was a symbiotic relationship, with the buzz and attendant publicity surrounding the TV show pumping up the record sales. Despite the early lead of the musical side of the band's business, the endurance would be tested over the second season and the show's eventual cancellation in 1968. The question then would be whether the musical side could survive on its own.

6

A Quartered Head

In this real-life episode the Monkees stage a revolution and take over the machine. This story takes place on January 27, 1967, in a bungalow infused with a dreamy, downy light, surrounded by the elaborate staging of an imported tropical landscape: banana plants, bougainvillea, hibiscus. Set-designed in the Mediterranean Revival style, the expansive buildings in the middle of 12 acres of greenery and pathways feature arches and verandas, a Hollywood-sized version of a colonial palatial mansion, only sprayed with unreal peachy pink and gaudy green, even striped in some parts, while other parts reflect the shimmers of the imperial pool. It is the Beverly Hills Hotel at 9641 Sunset Boulevard, only a mile or so from the Strip but symbolic miles from the pop-rock scene, one of the "squarest" places in Los Angeles. Still, the ostentatious dream factory architecture and topiary offered the perfect setting for a palace revolt. Gathered in the bungalow for a meeting with Don Kirshner, the Monkees flipped the script, voicing on their own a concerted objection to their management.[1]

With the show doing well, a few live appearances under their belt, two smash singles, and a hit album, Kirshner expected an appreciative audience, though he had heard some stirrings of discontent. After all, Kirshner had put together a follow-up album, *More of the Monkees*, released only a few weeks earlier (January 9) to certified success, hitting retail shelves already as a qualified gold record by the Recording Industry Association of America for preorders. Awed by the incredible success of their first album and single, Kirshner had rushed to put out this second record. He could assemble the album quickly as his production team—Boyce and Hart, Jack Keller, Jeff Barry, and others—had stockpiled songs from the summer sessions and occasional sessions over the fall. As on the first album, Kirshner placed his name right below the record's title on the back cover, in bold letters: "Music Supervision: Don Kirshner." Below his name you find the beguiling and revealing credit: "Music Coordinators: Lester Sill-Emil LaViola." Not in bold. But a revelation of Kirshner's managerial system: Sill did much of the supervision or coordination on this album, given its heavy reliance on the recordings from the summer of 1966 under the producers Boyce and Hart and Jack Keller. Indeed, all kinds of asterisks dotted the song listing, leading close readers down to an inventory of no fewer than eight different producers for the album's twelve songs: Tommy Boyce and Bobby Hart, Neil Sedaka and Carole Bayer, Jeff Barry and Jack Keller, Jeff Barry on his own, Jeff Barry working with Gerry Goffin and Carole King, and even Michael Nesmith on two of the tracks.

If his bold "Music Supervision" credit failed to signal who stood in charge of the project, the liner notes made it clear. Kirshner wrote them in the first person, and signed it as "President, Colgems Records, a Division of Columbia Pictures and Screen Gems TV." Yet he presented the production as a family affair, crediting the songwriters, the boys themselves, and the whole team from Schneider and Rafelson to executives at Screen Gems TV and RCA Victor:

> After the Monkees' first single record and album both reached No. 1 on the charts, it became difficult for anyone to be objective about their tremendous talents. With the second single climbing for the No. 1 spot, I thought I'd ask some of the greatest contemporary songwriters and record producers their opinions of the Monkees.

So I asked . . .

Gerry Goffin and Carole King who wrote Go Away, Little Girl

Tommy Boyce and Bobby Hart, the authors of Last Train to Clarksville

Jeff Barry who produced I'm a Believer

Neil Sedaka, the well-known artist and composer

Carole Bayer who wrote the lyrics for A Groovy Kind of Love

Neil Diamond who penned Cherry, Cherry

Jack Keller who wrote the music for Run to Him

Sandy Linzer and Denny Rendell, the authors of A Lover's Concerto

Roger Atkins who wrote the lyrics to It's My Life

Ben Raleigh who wrote the words to Love Is a Hurtin' Thing

Some of Kirshner's narrative involved revisionism in the service of public relations: many, like Boyce and Hart, had already made their contributions to the album before Kirshner's haste to assemble it. Others, like Jeff Barry or Neil Diamond, really did receive a call and responded with creative contributions (to put it mildly: "I'm a Believer," after all). To this list of talent, Kirshner added: "The versatility and talents of The Monkees, both individually and collectively, burst forth here."

The distinction between individual and collective contributions probably struck a nerve with some in the band: Nesmith contributed two songs to the record, but missed a mention on Kirshner's list of songwriters. Neither could any Monkee recognize "collective" contributions by the band at this point. Session musicians dominated all the tracks; some even recorded in New York studios with vocal overdubs added in Hollywood. Still, Kirshner heaped on the praise of the band members at this point:

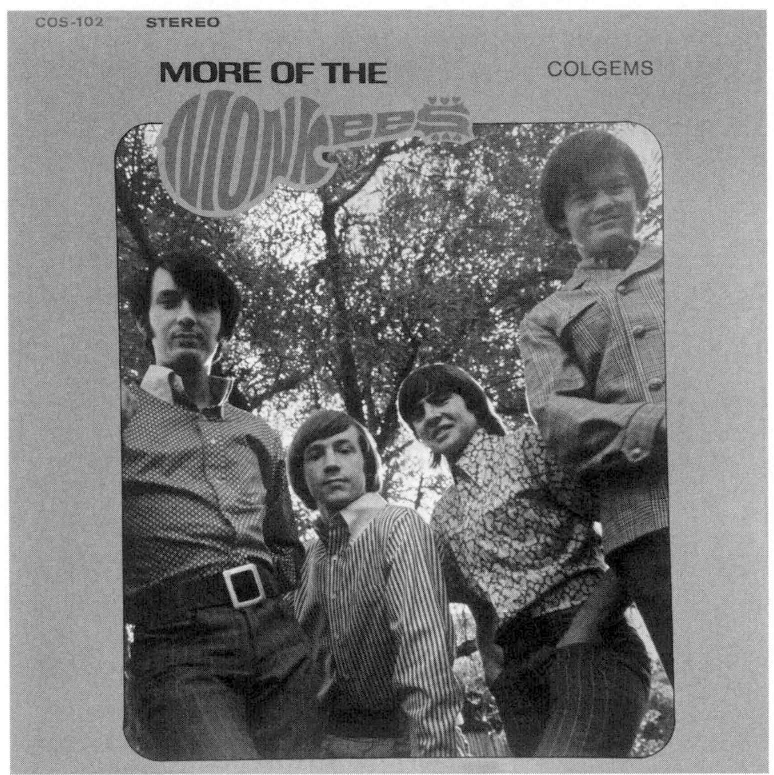

The record that spawned a revolt.

> The performances of Micky as an artist on I'm a Believer and (I'm Not Your) Steppin' Stone; Michael as a producer and composer of Mary, Mary and as an artist, writer, and producer on The Kind of Girl I Could Love; David's vocal interpretation on Look Out (Here Comes Tomorrow); and Peter's unique performance of Your Auntie Grizelda are but the beginnings of the great recordings yet to be done by the boys.

Generous praise of the individual members. A closer reading, which any of the band could decipher, hints at their limited involvement in the recordings: Davy and Micky on vocals, clearly, Michael as

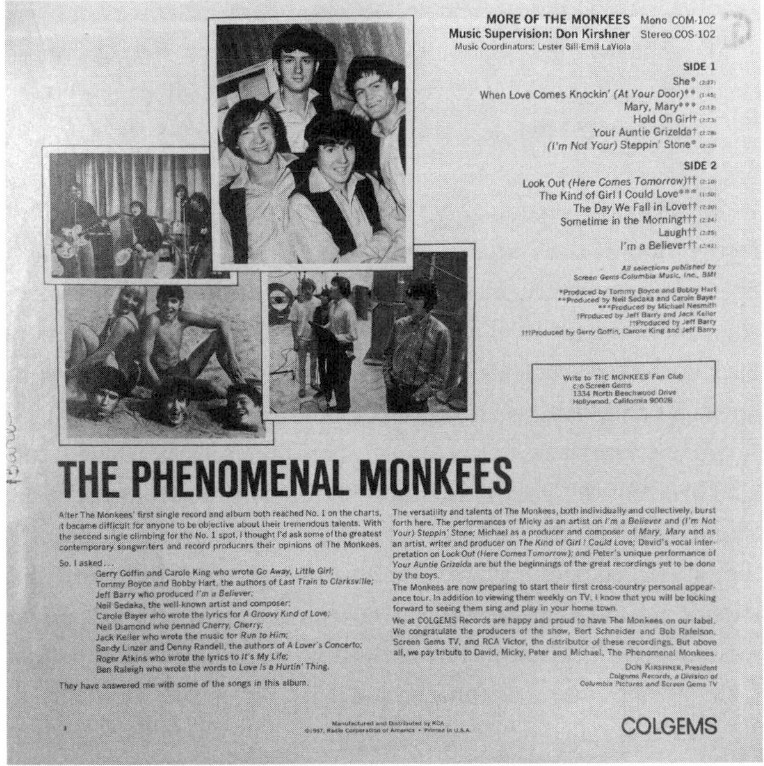

MORE OF THE MONKEES Mono COM-102
Music Supervision: Don Kirshner Stereo COS-102
Music Coordinators: Lester Sill-Emil LaViola

SIDE 1

She* (2:37)
When Love Comes Knockin' *(At Your Door)*** (1:45)
Mary, Mary*** (2:12)
Hold On Girl† (2:23)
Your Auntie Grizelda† (2:28)
(I'm Not Your) Steppin' Stone* (2:25)

SIDE 2

Look Out *(Here Comes Tomorrow)*†† (2:10)
The Kind of Girl I Could Love*** (1:50)
The Day We Fall in Love†† (2:20)
Sometime in the Morning††† (2:24)
Laugh†† (2:25)
I'm a Believer†† (2:41)

All selections published by
Screen Gems-Columbia Music, Inc., BMI

*Produced by Tommy Boyce and Bobby Hart
**Produced by Neil Sedaka and Carole Bayer
***Produced by Michael Nesmith
†Produced by Jeff Barry and Jack Keller
††Produced by Jeff Barry
†††Produced by Gerry Goffin, Carole King and Jeff Barry

Write to THE MONKEES Fan Club
c/o Screen Gems
1334 North Beechwood Drive
Hollywood, California 90028

THE PHENOMENAL MONKEES

After The Monkees' first single record and album both reached No. 1 on the charts, it became difficult for anyone to be objective about their tremendous talents. With the second single climbing for the No. 1 spot, I thought I'd ask some of the greatest contemporary songwriters and record producers their opinions of The Monkees.

So, I asked . . .

Gerry Goffin and Carole King who wrote *Go Away, Little Girl*;
Tommy Boyce and Bobby Hart, the authors of *Last Train to Clarksville*;
Jeff Barry who produced *I'm a Believer*;
Neil Sedaka, the well-known artist and composer;
Carole Bayer who wrote the lyrics for *A Groovy Kind of Love*;
Neil Diamond who penned *Cherry, Cherry*;
Jack Keller who wrote the music for *Run to Him*;
Sandy Linzer and Denny Randell, the authors of *A Lover's Concerto*;
Roger Atkins who wrote the lyrics to *It's My Life*;
Ben Raleigh who wrote the words to *Love Is a Hurtin' Thing*.

They have answered me with some of the songs in this album.

The versatility and talents of The Monkees, both individually and collectively, burst forth here. The performances of Micky as an artist on *I'm a Believer* and *(I'm Not Your) Steppin' Stone*; Michael as a producer and composer of *Mary, Mary* and as an artist, writer and producer on *The Kind of Girl I Could Love*; David's vocal interpretation on *Look Out (Here Comes Tomorrow)*; and Peter's unique performance of *Your Auntie Grizelda* are but the beginnings of the great recordings yet to be done by the boys.

The Monkees are now preparing to start their first cross-country personal appearance tour. In addition to viewing them weekly on TV, I know that you will be looking forward to seeing them sing and play in your home town.

We at COLGEMS Records are happy and proud to have The Monkees on our label. We congratulate the producers of the show, Bert Schneider and Bob Rafelson, Screen Gems TV, and RCA Victor, the distributor of these recordings. But above all, we pay tribute to David, Micky, Peter and Michael, The Phenomenal Monkees.

Don Kirshner, President
Colgems Records, a Division of Columbia Pictures and Screen Gems TV

Manufactured and Distributed by RCA
©1967, Radio Corporation of America • Printed in U.S.A.

COLGEMS

Kirshner pulls back the curtain.

composer and producer—steps up in public recognition regarding the first album, but no indication of his musical performance—and barely a nod for Peter (a "unique performance"?). Kirshner framed it all as praise, but for the band members, some balking at their hemmed-in roles in the Monkees machine, the hype must have stung.

Kirshner ended his liner notes by highlighting the managerial work behind the band's productions, which embroiled Nesmith and Tork in a question of legitimacy:

> We at Colgems Records are happy and proud to have The Monkees on our label. We congratulate the producers of the

> show, Bert Schneider and Bob Rafelson, Screen Gems TV, and RCA Victor, the distributor of these recordings. But, above all, we pay tribute to David, Micky, Peter and Michael, The Phenomenal Monkees.

It was a diplomatic note to close on and, just as graciously, a recognition of the system, which often goes unacknowledged on liner notes, publicity, and journalism on the industry, an acknowledgment of the teams of workers that supported this phenomenon. Back at the Beverly Hills Hotel, Kirshner held even more gracious notes: fat checks for each Monkee.

At any rate, none of the Monkees read the liner notes with this kind of attention. They were simply shocked by the existence of the album at all, for no one had informed them of its release. Apparently, they stumbled across a copy at a record store while on tour. Their attention to the album's cardboard cover focused entirely on its front: what they saw as a lame picture of the band pulled from a photo shoot for a JCPenney line of clothing branded to their image. They hated it.

Nesmith called it "the worst album ever." It sold like bananas. It quickly swapped out their first album in the No. 1 spot, where it had remained as late as January. More than that, *More of the Monkees* maintained its No. 1 position for an astounding eighteen weeks. Adding up the streak with the first album, the two records topped the charts for 31 weeks. Moreover, the first album rested at No. 2 while *More* held its top spot.

It's true that the new recording lacked consistency, sonically and thematically. Too many songs just don't fit the flow of the album. The garage rock mashers "She" and "Steppin' Stone" open and close side one like booming blasts across the bow, echoing each other with their wailing chants and pounding, jerking beats. "When Love Comes Knocking at Your Door" comes right after "She" and knocks the energy down to zero. Sonically the overly trebled number—tinny guitar and Davy's drained double-tracked vocals (also pushed up too much in front of the mix)—jars with the rich bass and depth of "She." Thematically, this trite Neil Sedaka cut also jars with its oldie tone and structure. This kind of wacky sequencing continues with almost every track on the album. The rollicking Nesmith number "Mary, Mary"—a better follow-up to "She"—leads to the wispy "Hold On Girl," only followed by the goofball "Auntie Grizelda." The last song's cowriter, Jack Keller, intended it as a social commentary (as in "Mother's Little Helper"), but it ended up with knee-slapping rhythm, overly nasal vocals by Peter, and goofy hiccups and vocal sound effects dominating the solo section. The mix is a muddy mess. And overall, most of the songs lack the sound of the band created by Boyce and Hart on the first album: the twangy guitar and bass, shimmering chords, and British Invasion pop vocalizations. Still, the disc contained cuts like "She," "Steppin' Stone," "Sometime in the Morning," "Mary, Mary," "Look Out (Here Comes Tomorrow)," and "I'm a Believer." Six bona fide classics (half the album's cuts).

On top of it all, Kirshner insisted on releasing "A Little Bit Me, A Little Bit You," a Diamond-penned production, as their next single. And he did so without consulting key RCA executives or management on the Monkees project. Nesmith pushed for his own composition, "The Girl I Knew Somewhere," as a potential 45, if not a B-side at the very least. Kirshner's initial printing of the single put "She Hangs Out" on the B-side, which he distributed to DJs, jumpstarting his own mini promotional campaign (rewind to review the math again for the record: "A Little Bit" hit No. 2; "The Girl I Knew Somewhere" No. 39 on the charts).

All these arguments swirled through the hot air in the Beverly Hills Hotel bungalow. Nesmith resented their lack of involvement in the recordings as well as their lack of say in the many decisions made around the band, from photo sessions to concerts to releases and album covers. He pushed for the Monkees themselves to play their own material on upcoming recordings, and mentioned the bad publicity suffered by the band over their made-to-order status and lack of musicianship. Kirshner countered with concerns over the band's lack of musical experience. He emphasized the commercial risk of releasing lesser material and the difficulty of recovering, in terms of reputation and momentum, from a flop or two.

When Nesmith confronted Kirshner with these issues, Kirshner deferred to his lawyer, who informed Nesmith of his contractual obligations to fall in line. Enraged, Nesmith went ape and apparently punched a wall (not a smart move for a guitarist, if this part of the story is true, though his hand apparently survived), exclaiming to Kirshner or his lawyer, "That could have been your face! #$%@*#$@#." A performance as good as any of his on the show.

The meeting ended with no resolution. All parties left in different states of mind. Tork probably sided with Nesmith, though he may have sensed that Nesmith really wanted to take control of the band (a sense that panned out over the course of the year). Jones and Dolenz understood all along that the band represented a fiction and that Kirshner and his team served them well in this regard. Nesmith recognized that his arrogance went too far and said as much in a reflective conversation later with Lester Sill.

Upper management—at RCA and Columbia Studios (Screen Gems)—maintained a commitment to the Monkees project. They needed to sustain the members of the band as they represented their investment. So they relieved Kirshner from his post as the head of Colgems Records and replaced him with Lester Sill. Kirshner sued, seeking damages totaling $35 million, accusing the owners of conspiring to interfere with and terminate his contractual rights and diminishing his reputation. Kirshner's firing and the lawsuit led to what one trade paper called "a most unusual case of corporate schizophrenia": Kirshner remained in charge of Columbia-Screen Gems Music, with a contract running for another nine years, and a $70,000 annual salary against 7½ percent of the pretax net profits.[2] Columbia filed counterclaims in federal court, enumerating the managerial oversteps on Kirshner's part (including the costs of reissuing the latest 45), and revealingly betrayed the internal tensions and anxiety permeating the band at this period around the issue of their authenticity:

> Kirshner caused or permitted to be issued self-adulatory publicity which was demeaning to the Monkees, which erroneously implied that the members of the Monkees whose talents plaintiff should have been developing and whose reputations he should have been fostering were lacking in talent, and which created in the minds of the public the false and misleading impression that plaintiff, through the use of electronics and other synthetic recording techniques, was solely responsible for the success of the Monkees' records and that the Monkees themselves made no real contribution to that success.[3]

This section of the claim reads more like notes from a group therapy session than legitimate or provable legal claims: "demeaning," "misleading," "reputations." When they fault Kirshner for failing to develop and foster their talent, it sounds more like bad parenting. In turn, Raybert and Colgems allowed the Monkees to take a measure of control over the recording of their next album that spring.

Most versions of this story render it as a scene of liberation, with the Monkees, led by their revolutionary Nesmith, freeing themselves of the autocracy of Kirshner and allowing themselves to work as a real band. A triumph of authenticity. A new beginning. And yet it added up to the beginning of the end. After a brief, shining moment—a nifty album, 1967's *Headquarters*, on which they played most of the instruments—and a strong follow-up that year, *Pisces, Aquarius, Capricorn & Jones Ltd.*, they returned to a more fragmented production process, arguably even less cohesive in planning than before.

Jeff Barry came back to work with the band. They recorded songs by Jack Keller, King and Goffin, Leiber and Stoller, more Boyce and Hart numbers, Sedaka and Bayer. Peter Tork appears on only a single track on the band's 1968 album, "Daydream Believer," which was recorded much earlier. As their new producer, Chip Douglas, reflected on this period: "Things were kind of falling apart and there was less and less time. Everybody was more and more frustrated and wanting to do their own ideas."[4]

Session musicians like Hal Blaine, Larry Knechtel, and Louie Shelton turned up again and again for their paychecks, as did session players new to the Monkees' team like Eddie Hoh or Kim Copli on drums. This post-revolutionary development led to the back-cover note on *The Birds, the Bees, and the Monkees*: "Our special thanks to the many talented musicians who performed with us and under our supervision on this album, [signed] The Monkees." They had to say it: "under our supervision." Whatever control they gained in the Beverly Hills Hotel uprising seemed more fragmented than their foundational period. So much for the revolution. To top it off, the TV show's ratings tumbled in the second season, leading to its early cancellation. Without the support of the TV show, their singles and concerts floundered. When they released a greatest hits collection in 1969, it barely made it to the Top 100 on the *Billboard* charts (from today's perspective it contains all the enduring classics)—by the numbers, their "greatest" represented their worst-selling album. By the end of 1968, Peter Tork quit the Monkees.

Then, in January 1970, the Monkees broke up. The next morning, the sun rose on the Los Angeles music industry, and the system continued its orbits. Studio musicians answered calls. Songwriters worked on their medium. Producers weighed the instrumentation, recording levels, and mixing for their artists. Recording engineers balanced these considerations with the available equipment and conditions of their studios. Club bookers auditioned new acts. Musicians looked for club dates or appointments with record or publishing companies. New aspirants met the day and pounded the pavement of Sunset Boulevard and its arteries in Hollywood.

Former Monkees session musician Glen Campbell had several hit albums and singles to his name, like 1968's classic "Wichita Lineman" and 1969's "True Grit"—he already had four Grammy awards on his shelf—and hosted his own TV variety show (he even hosted the Monkees as guests before they split up). Carole King was on the verge of launching her own tremendously successful career as a solo artist, stitching together *Tapestry* in 1971 and its string of hits. Neil Diamond was already on his way, scoring No. 1 hits as an artist on his own in 1970 and 1972. Louie Shelton, a steady contributor to the early Monkees sessions, continued work as a session guitarist, taping hours of recordings with John Lennon, Barbra Streisand, Stevie Wonder, Boz Scaggs, and basically the whole phone book of pop and rock stars. He soon moved into the producer's chair, scoring major hits with acts like Seals and Crofts. Session bassist Larry Taylor bounced along with the rise of Canned Heat and their hit "Going Up the Country," going all the way up to the stage at Woodstock. Lester Sill remained in his new position as Kirshner's replacement for over two decades. Boyce and Hart launched their own careers as an act with a record deal and tours, though it never took off. Other session musicians clocked in the hours and added up the years on their careers.

Kirshner moved on from the Monkees to a project that immediately scored, on the scale of moola and schadenfreude. Don Kirshner Music, Inc. produced 1969's chart-topping confection "Sugar, Sugar," a saccharine sensation of a single sticking at No. 1 for four weeks and on the charts for almost half of the year: the year's biggest single, selling millions, a chewy bubblegum number morphing into solid gold. Credited to the Archies, a nonexistent band composed of TV cartoon characters, it was performed by a group of session musicians and singers who spit it out under the production (and cowriting) of Jeff Barry, who helmed "I'm a Believer," "A Little Bit Me, A Little Bit You," and some of Neil Diamond's solo work. And the song mined much from Diamond's method: a soulful, slow-burn verse delivered

Sweet, sweet schadenfreude for Kirshner, however short-lived.

with breathy singing before finding joyous, infectious release in a gospel sing-along catchy chorus.

In the tales surrounding the Monkees' rebellion against Kirshner, "Sugar, Sugar" often surfaces as a grace note coda for the disgraced Kirshner, a small victory following his unceremonious ousting (in some mythic versions of this story, Kirshner initially offers the song to the Monkees, who refuse it). Studio musicians. A made-to-order TV band. Jeff Barry spinning the recording knobs. Kirshner was with friends again. And back on top. Chew on that, Monkees!

But the schadenfreude proved short-lived. A bigger cartoon gummed up the works in 1970 when Kirshner attempted to directly replicate the Monkees project on a grander scale: a cinematic multiracial made-to-order band, scouted from around the world, in partnership with 007 film producer Harry Saltzman, who would produce the accompanying film launching the act. The band (and film) was called Tomorrow, though they never saw the light of day as musical performers. After the film and its soundtrack flopped, the team called it a day, scrapping any tomorrow plans for further recordings or performances (one of the band members, Olivia Newton-John, at least launched a successful solo career).[5]

The Monkees' banana republic rebellion broke them free of Kirshner. Yet their freedom came at the upper levels of the system. They still retained a recording contract; a managerial team that advised them on their recordings, personal appearances, and concert tours; a television series that helped promote their records; a public relations team that landed them articles in teenybopper magazines and even legitimate rags. It remains questionable, if not unbelievable, to call this move a triumph of authenticity. The real story is that the question of authenticity wormed its way into the band and corroded it from within.

When the band took control over the recording process for their next album in the spring of 1967, they discovered the producer through the networks of the music business in Los Angeles, following a typical path in the system and its ecosystems. Nesmith met Chip Douglas, then a bassist with the Turtles, at a show at the Sunset Strip's Whisky a Go Go, and asked him to work as their producer. Douglas had impressed Nesmith with his arrangements on the Turtles' monster hit "Happy Together." A relative novice in the production booth, Douglas's leap was not too uncommon, given his musical chops and arranging skills, and he worked with an experienced engineer, the great Hank Cicalo. So, that spring in RCA's Hollywood recording studios, they all set to work on an album with (mostly) Monkees behind the instruments and Douglas and Cicalo guiding them all from the studio booth.

Headquarters, the result of their efforts, "should have been a disaster, DIY at best," as the critic Bob Stanley notes, instead of "quite the most morning-fresh album of the era, with tinges of country and folk rock and a tangible sense of gleeful freedom."[6] The Monkees turned in strong performances on the songs, and they wrote quite a few of their own. *Headquarters* celebrates the pluralism of popular music—with tracks ranging from the emerging genre of country-rock to vaudeville flavors to pop-rock to jazzy pop to pop-folk. The album refused to take a monolithic commercial approach of simply replicating a successful formula. It opted, instead, to engage with the pluralism of Top 40, which could broadcast a range of different hits in different genres at any moment, and, of course, the pluralism of their model: the Beatles. That aspect of the emulation of the Beatles remains an important and incisive explanation of the success of the Monkees—it's an insight that escaped many imitators. Focusing

Revolutions per Monkees; yet still rocking department-store-style clothing.

on this Beatlesque trait amounted to a celebration of eclecticism, a utopian inclusiveness. Ironically, the cover of this post-revolutionary album featured the foursome in tacky JCPenney clothes. But the songs stretched beyond that. Douglas's production remained a little thin sonically even while it included jazz-inflected tunes like "Forget That Girl," echoing the pop-jazz of the Zombies, or somber songs with serene mixing and arrangements like "Shades of Gray" (with shades of Simon and Garfunkel).

The back of the album featured a patchwork of pictures depicting the boys during the recording process, a conventional collage that sought to capture the kind of back-cover imagery of more legitimate bands—almost every major band in the mid-1960s rocked the same photo spread on their back covers. In this case, we see the band members consulting each other around their instruments and with clear recording studio *mise-en-scène* in the background. Davy plays the tambourine. Micky behind the drumkit. Peter at the piano. Michael pointing like a conductor with the guitar strapped around him and headphones mounting his moptop. At the top left corner, the cover modestly if still insistently let the listener know: "We aren't the only musicians on this album, but the occasional extra bass or horn player played under our direction, so that this is all ours." Then the note got a little more defensive: "Each one of us has some musical thing, from Manchester to Texas, from the East Coast to the West, and when four people just go with their thing, what comes out is a whole."

Adding up the whole proved a little more difficult. Of the twelve songs, three came from Nesmith. Peter Tork delivered one (working with Joseph Richards) and Dolenz another. All nifty tunes. The others came from the Kirshner stable: three from Boyce and Hart, one from Jack Keller, another from Barry Mann and Cynthia Weil. Chip Douglas punched up many of the songs with his robust bass playing. He also oversaw take after take of Dolenz on the drums to get him up to speed and even had to splice tapes together to

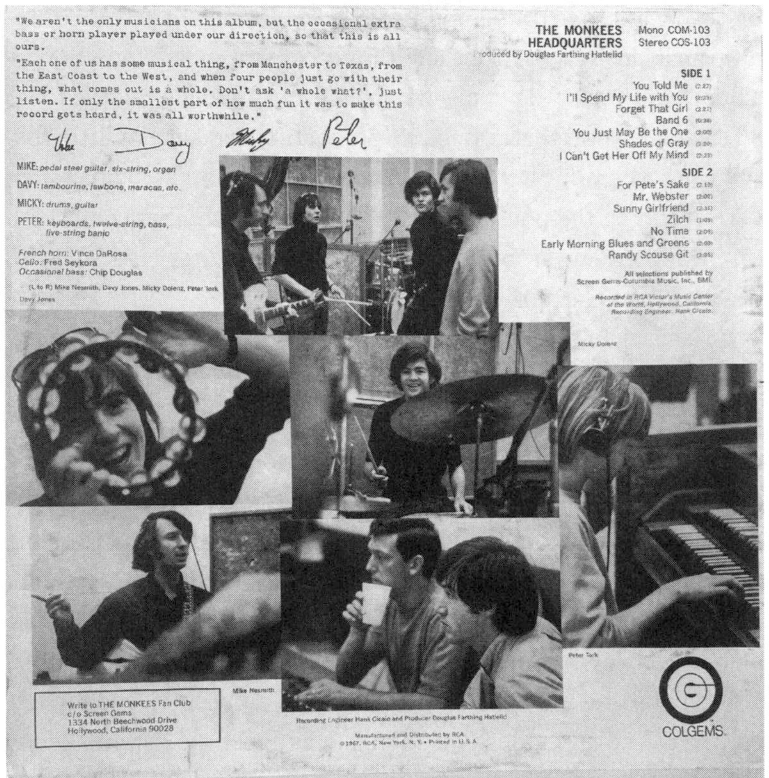

Documenting their production process: back cover photographic motifs, like a real band.

get the right sound out of the novice. As a project and a statement, *Headquarters* plays off authenticity. In the production of this album the band sought to rupture their prefabricated world. Yet the authenticity here remains complicated. They launched the album, after all, from a privileged position with scaffolding engineered by their management team. The very system they rebelled against put them in the place to indulge in creating this album—and they nonetheless relied on a slew of songwriters.

Still, the Monkees and their team went on a campaign to validate their newly won artistic control, informing journalists and others in the business of the process behind this new album project and encouraging all to spread the word. A May 23, 1967, internal memo at LA's KHJ radio from their program director Ron Jacobs informs his Boss Jocks: "On this album, by the way, they do all the singing and playing and, in addition, most of the tunes on the album were composed by miscellaneous Monkees." At the same time, however, Jacobs warns them to temper any hype around the band: "Effective as of Sunday morning when the sign was removed, there are no further specific requirements regarding Monkee LP airplay. There are three tunes from their album on the playlist . . . play them when appropriate and if requested. In other words, we do not wish to over-do airplay of Monkees songs . . . play only what is justified." The Monkees would have to swing it on their own. And they did: though the album generated no singles, it achieved their third No. 1 slot in a row, three for three so far.

"Once the Monkees took control of their recording career it got steadily worse," their new music supervisor Lester Sill reflected a few decades later.[7] Their subsequent albums rode on their earlier momentum initially, but then started to drop. Their concert tours in 1967 jammed in audiences. But by late 1968 and early 1969, their short tours featured half-filled auditoriums or smaller venues, and even forced cancellations for lack of sales. Moreover, they returned to many of the songwriters enlisted for them by the Kirshner period: Boyce and Hart, Goffin and King, Leiber and Stoller. The *Pisces* album offered a few Nesmith songs on side two, but that's it. *Birds*, the next year's album, turned up a few more. But other songwriters filled out the rest of their albums.

Yet during this period the Monkees still produced "Daydream Believer, "Cuddly Toy," "Tapioca Tundra" (an interesting Nesmith composition), and songs like "Words" or "Valleri," holdovers from their earliest productive period. Nesmith dropped several great tunes onto albums during this period. But many of these few great songs from this time came from other writers, acknowledging the platform of support that propelled the band to their initial success.

Their last major hit—1967's "Daydream Believer," written by John Stewart—developed from a stirring and simple set of verses into a rousing uplifting bridge and chorus, enhancing the elation through rich instrumentation that builds into a cinematic wave, a sunny recording laced with a trace of melancholy. It echoes the cheerful buoyancy of Chip Douglas's production on the Turtles' "Happy Together," inhabiting a West Coast spirit with its spacious moves and whistling hypnotic refrain. Shorty Rogers handled the arrangements, even lifting the same seven-note phrase preceding the chorus on the Beach Boys' "Help Me, Rhonda." Aside from the musical contributions of two Monkees (Tork on piano, Nesmith on guitar), Douglas worked the session like the early recordings: studio musicians on every other instrument.

Despite the Monkees' revolution, they even eventually parted ways with Chip Douglas over conflicts with Nesmith, returning their albums to teams of producers. Nesmith only seemed interested in getting a few songs on forthcoming albums for the royalty stream. "When we were doing *Pisces*," Chip Douglas reflected, "Mike would come in with three songs . . . he knew that he was making a lot of money if he got his original songs on there." Douglas recalls Nesmith being enthusiastic and cooperative while working on those numbers. Then he'd refuse to work on other songs.[8]

One of the biggest steps the Monkees' team took in this period—and the biggest flop—was their movie debut, *Head*, in 1968. Since the whole project of the Monkees as a TV show sutured with actual record releases started with the inspiration of *A Hard Day's Night*, itself a merger of music and film (though the musical component in that case got going on its own and by its own), a movie was inevitable: indeed, a prospect from the start of the whole plan. The management team at Raybert drove this entire part of the Monkeemobile. Both Rafelson and Schneider maintained ambitions to get into the movie business, especially now that a "New Hollywood" culture emerged, with films like *The Graduate* and

Bonnie and Clyde capturing the top spots of the box-office draws and the youth market at the same time. Management then drove this ill-conceived concept to take a teenybopper boob-tube band into the new cinema of violence and sexuality characterizing the "New Hollywood." They convinced (or coerced) the band to take on Rafelson's—a first-time feature film director—wild, experimental production of *Head*: an R-rated artwork targeted to the counterculture, a mismatch in both directions. A cynical film that took on the Vietnam War and the entertainment business by appropriating techniques from every other experimental film at the time, it featured graphic newsreel footage of the war, old clips from Hollywood films, and already dated bizarre visual effects. Though released in the heyday of the new movement—the same year as *2001: A Space Odyssey* and *Petulia*, to take only a few examples—the film paled in comparison in its disparate episodic experiments.

Even early in the decision to go with this direction for the film, the management team sensed some trouble. Apparently, they sought out the advice of Marshall McLuhan, at that time a Fordham professor and a hyped-up media guru seen as hip to the latest trends in media. Only his assistant answered the query from the Monkees' team, which asked about selling the movie while their appeal appeared on the wane. His surprising but revealing answer: "The best thing is don't tell anybody the Monkees are in the movie."[9]

The film's exploitation strategy sought to capitalize on counterculture tropes, hoping these tactics would sell the film and simultaneously lend it some legitimacy with the counterculture itself. "Two Unique 'Head' Campaigns Reach Audiences at Every Level," one of their promotional pamphlets read: "For the 'Modern' Film Audience!" and "For the Monkees Fans!," an impossible task according to McLuhan's minion. The first strategy encouraged theater owners to use ads "wherever 'Hip' crowds gather: local discotheques, women's mod fashion shops, . . . [even, believe it or not] libraries, high school and college spas." Or, better yet: "Put a psychedelic light show into your lobby, well in advance of playdate, then a color-wheel and flasher light . . . Girls compete for best 'Head' styles." It even encouraged theater owners to hire a local to dress up like "a guru, an East Indian religious teacher," with long hair, a beard, and a long, flowing robe.[10]

Guru or no guru, color wheels or no psychedelic lobbies, the movie flopped both commercially and critically. Renata Adler at the *New York Times* called it "dreadfully written," the mildest of her comments in characterizing the film as a mixture of pot and advertising:

> The Monkees, who are among the least-talented contemporary music groups and know it, are most interesting for their lack of similarity to The Beatles. Going through ersatz Beatle songs, and jokes and motions, their complete lack of distinction of any kind—the fact that fame was stamped on them by hucksters as it might have been on any nice four random, utterly undistinguished boys—makes their performance modest and almost brave.[11]

The soundtrack's only single, "Porpoise Song," a late stab at psychedelia, never got above water, gasping for air at No. 62 on *Billboard*, but sank like a stone within a month.

Even before the porpoise failed to peak, their first single of 1968 failed to crack the Top 10, barely tipping over the Top 20 (No. 19 was the best it could do). They released "D. W. Washburn" as a single for the first time following the end of the TV show, so its lack of heavy promotion may account for its modest charting and sales. However, the choice of material may explain its failure as well. Lester Sill picked an old Leiber and Stoller tune that seemed out of sync with the times.

The curtain fell swiftly and forcefully. After the show's cancellation and some stumbling on the record charts, the biggest sign of the changing times came in the empty seats and stadiums for their latest concerts. Half-filled venues. Cancelled shows. When *Rolling Stone* deemed the band worthy of some coverage, it reviewed one of their gigs at the Oakland Coliseum, noting a crowd of about 1,500 or 2,000 in a venue that could hold almost 30,000. A Colgems promotions executive spilled the beans publicly to a trade press reporter: "I've watched their rise and demise. The wheel has turned full cycle. Let's face it, the group was a phenomenon in 1967; now they'll have to rebuild."[12]

It would be cute to say that the system turned against them. In fact, the system just followed its course in sorting out hits from flops. You can say that a management problem disrupted their operations. Kirshner wielded his supervision too forcefully and independently when he released the single "A Little Bit Me, a Little Bit You," and did so without consultation with the management team supporting the band. Likewise, Nesmith arrogantly assumed that the success achieved by the band at this point would allow them to take the reins. The clash came about through managerial conflict on both sides, with Schneider and Rafelson siding with Nesmith under the misconception that this represented the will of the entire band. Indeed, Jones and Dolenz remained much more apprehensive about uncoupling from Kirshner. This confusion or lack of true cohesion in the managerial plans comes out in the productions that followed *Headquarters*.

The new FM radio culture dialed in with the new rock criticism in its valorization of free form approaches, experimentation, and individual artistic expression. In fact, FM promotor, DJ, and programmer Tom Donahue promoted the new format in an excoriating piece published in 1967 in *Rolling Stone* magazine. Donahue picked up on the new rock culture, lauding its authenticity and innovation as an evolving medium by attacking what he called "the biggest deterrent to the progress, expansion, and success of contemporary music": Top 40 radio.[13] That format, with its "carefully scanned . . . sales figures," failed to recognize that "music has matured, [and] the audience has matured." That failure opened the door to the new format he pushed on FM radio. His message radiated through the underground, college radio, the new rock journalism, other FM stations, and even the industry. *Billboard* in 1967 reported that "KMPX-FM's Donahue Programs Music with a Wide Open View," quoting the FM proselytizer. "There's no restriction on the deejay."[14] As a noted rock critic picked up on these waves, he described both the new music acts and the FM DJs as "poets who are reflecting a new attitude which demands a new form of presentation on the air."[15]

The management attempted to tap into this new market with the release of the *Head* soundtrack. In promotional material addressed to retailers and their regional promotional teams, Colgems noted that "in addition to the AM and FM Stations across the country, the 'Head' album was serviced to all college and underground stations."[16] That part of the campaign failed as the band could not live down its earlier incarnation as a genuinely successful Top 40 band.

Moreover, the Monkees were outliving their demographic of preteens, who were moving on to other material, trends the Monkees could not convincingly join, both in terms of their management team and their previous associations as a manufactured band and their TV image. As the *Gavin Report* fretted as early as 1966:

> Top 40 programmers once assumed that teens would tune their way. Not now. Many 15 to 18 year olds aren't tuning into any stations very often; they're listening to their favorite LP's on their record players. We must realize that these middle and upper teens have different tastes than their younger brothers and sisters. Pop formatters should make special efforts to regain and hold the senior high school group, not just by playing more LP material, but by special promos.[17]

Internal memos at KHJ recognize this shift and strategized to add more album cuts to their playlists.

Another response by AM radio came in the form of audio histories of rock, with KHJ leading the way in 1967. These programs appealed to the studious, thoughtful listener allegedly characterizing the FM audience in pop and rock discourse by approaching the medium as a form of art history, covering its foundations, its innovations, and its development. KRLA picked up on this approach and created their own episodic historical survey, *Pop Chronicles*, which aired in 1969. And in this case, we can say that the system, or this part of it, did, indeed, attack or critically interrogate the Monkees project.

Pop Chronicles devoted part of an episode to the Monkees and the problem of their manufactured status with eviscerating commentary. The music critic Pete Johnson led the way by questioning the whole process of putting together a band to appear suddenly at the same level as Cream, the Beatles, or the Kinks, fully fledged groups with a history of work behind their achievements. To underscore his skepticism, he mocked the number of producers on their second album: "that's more producers than songs on the album." With less scorn, Phil Spector gently dissected the Monkees. "The reason people don't like the Monkees," the music maestro hissed with surprising empathy, "is because they didn't pay their dues," articulating the primary issue with this manufactured band: the lack of an origin story outside of the industrial machinations that supported them. Spector accurately speculated on how hard this must be on the Monkees—he called it "a traumatic experience"—living with the knowledge of their fabrication and related lack of respect from their artistic community.

Surprisingly, Nesmith himself went on the program to defend the band. Though he often presented himself as the whistleblower or Monkees muckraker, and the cantankerous prankster on the phoniness of the whole project, Nesmith just as often robustly defended the group, no more so than in this period. He would go back and forth on these tactics, spilling out "the truth" to one journalist or defending the Monkees to another—sometimes in the same interview. The cross-purposes came out in this episode of the *Pop Chronicles*, with Nesmith shifting gears as he spoke. He admitted that the band lacked the talent of other groups, and that this fact limited any potential growth on their part. Regarding criticism of the Monkees, Nesmith declared: "The first thing for me to say is that I never have cared." Only to immediately flip sides and play a different tune: "But that's not true. It's been a source of great displeasure to me and immense discomfort. And I don't know why I should put that much stock in what Richard Goldstein says or whether *Crawdaddy!* ignores us or not," Nesmith continued candidly. "But they do and that upsets me. I would like them to like us and, I don't know; I guess it's because I'm an artist and my ego gets hurt."[18] Nesmith, then, confirmed Spector's suspicions about the corrosive effect the whole project had on the band. Moreover, Nesmith's commentary revealed the significant and swift influence rock criticism developed at this time (and that artists like Nesmith paid attention to them).

Nesmith played both tunes—naysayer and defender—in almost every encounter with the press at this time. *Flip* magazine, for example, ran a story in December 1968 titled "Mike Nesmith Tells It Like It Really Is!" He sought to expose the whole machinery as a way of salvaging and protecting his own reputation. His campaign gained little traction. For one thing, his revelations were no revelation to most readers. For another, the press had moved on from the band. *Tiger Beat* faded out its "I Visit the Monkees" column (replaced with "I Visit the Stars"); rising young pop singer Bobby Sherman got all the coverage now.[19]

On the campaign trail for cultural cachet, Nesmith funded the recording of his own mix of country-fused jazz, jazzified country, or brass band bomp, *The Wichita Train Whistle Sings*, an album of instrumental versions of his songs (all previously released). Instrumental versions as in ten trumpets, ten trombones, ten saxophones, five percussionists, four pianos, seven guitars, two drummers, and so on. The works. Nesmith apparently cut his own checks for two days of recording sessions at his stomping ground of Hollywood's RCA Studios with fifty-something musicians, seasoned sessioners like Hal Blaine, Larry Knechtel, and many old pals from the Monkees' sessions (though Nesmith was rarely in the same room for those recordings). Nesmith hired Shorty Rogers to arrange the songs entirely as all musical numbers no less, stripped of their lyrics (and therefore stripped of much chance of scoring a radio hit). It earned some respect—the lone critics who heard it here and there offered praise, including the great jazz critic Leonard Feather in an effusive appraisal in the *Los Angeles Times*. The charts offered silence. The burgeoning rock press ignored it, maintaining their assault on all things Monkees. "Everybody deserted us," Nesmith wailed on *Pop Chronicles*. "I sound like a martyr now," he added. "Maybe I am. Maybe I'm rightfully a martyr." Making martyrs worse, the Monkee ignored the fact that most critics attacked them from the start.

The new rock criticism spread from the *San Francisco Chronicle*'s Ralph Gleason (who helped Jann Wenner found *Rolling Stone*), *Crawdaddy!*, and Richard Goldstein's Pop Eye column in the *Village Voice*, started in 1965, and then to established journals like *Life*, the *New Yorker*, the *Saturday Review*, and *Esquire*, skating on the New Journalism, the pop sensibility infecting the 1960s, and the New Sensibility recognized by Susan Sontag, an effort to dethrone the seriousness of the establishment. But all of these critics unified around a vision of rock as an authentic form of personal expression, measuring artists by their commitment to such a vision.

Like any mythology or religion, the new rock criticism placed extreme emphasis on origins. Tracing an icon's roots became a sacral measure of its authenticity, as in religious stories, mythologies, and the new rock discourse (indeed, it became part of a band's public relations). The Monkees emerged just at this moment, which is precisely what makes them continually compelling, fascinating, and divisive. They are a product—a culmination—of the pop-rock industry as it became both a complex system of industrial practices and an image of the values that informed the rock mythos: spontaneity, utopianism, liberalism.

How many fans cared about the origin story of a song that turned them on? There is no way to measure an answer to that question. It depended on the listener's allegiance to the emerging rock mythos or to their more casual sense of fun. But the industry cared and clearly understood that enough fans were invested in this mythos. More importantly, the industry's emerging powerful sanctifiers—the new rock critics—cared and authenticated a musician based on this mythos as much as upon the music.

The origin story. Every band or pop star had to have one. You needed one as much as the elusive drummer or bass player to form a band, like any superhero. Both Spider-Man and Dylan had origin stories (Spidey's was a little more stable). The origin story might touch hallowed elements like the blues, folk, and R&B. It could include sacral touchstones like influences from sanctified icons such as Muddy Waters or Woody Guthrie. The narrative might include testing rites of passage like years spent in small clubs and low tours. It often included a lyrical and exegetical testament of opposition to mainstream, an affirmation of countercultural values. Origin stories accompanied the musicians like their equipment, clothes, images, and repertoire. Almost every article repeated these stories. Liner notes on albums often reiterated the origin stories in some way. Even (perhaps especially) rock's most romantic, Nietzschean canonizers like *Crawdaddy!*'s Richard Meltzer understood the deliverance of an origin story. In his almost hallucinogenic 1970 book, *Aesthetics of Rock*, a rambling treatise on the liberating force of rock as an art form, Meltzer outlines a literary diagram of a typical origin story for a band, his Romanticism flipping to a sly cynicism: "While other groups were turning out carbon copies, each fighting the other for the same identical sound, the ______________ decided to be different and daring. Then in August 1963 they cut their first record, ______________. It was a sensation overnight, zooming straight." Fill in the blanks. Every aspiring rock star wanted to sign their name on that line, to join that syntactical system, all spelled out and handled by the industry.

The authentic origin story protected a band from the transparent commercial work on the part of their record company and management. Fans understood the logic behind promotional advertising, billboards, radio commercials, and TV appearances. They understood that all kinds of handlers and managers worked with their favored bands or artists. You could even find songs about these aspects of the industry: the Byrds produced "So You Want to Be a Rock 'n' Roll Star" (rumored to be about the Monkees, but just as likely about their own experiences) and the Stones' "The Under Assistant West-Coast Promotion Man." But an origin story, among other factors like personal interviews or honest songwriting, created a kind of preindustrial persona for the artists. It rooted their artistic expression in a moment that stood out or aside from the machinations of the biz. For all their success stemming from almost every component and barometer of the pop system, the Monkees lacked the organic roots of an origin story, the seeming shield against the commercial fabrications of the industry.

Like Nesmith, Monkees' fans employ a weighty barrel of rhetorical devices to defend the band on the scale of authenticity. Each argument pleads to garner the Monkees their proper and earned appreciation. Each one comes with problems. One argument points to an act like the Supremes, who, without playing their own instruments or writing their own songs, still command respect and admiration for their artistry while averting the question of authenticity. This comparison breaks down over the fact that the Monkees, unlike the Supremes, initially waffled on the actual arrangements of their songs or made a mockery of the issue. In other words, the Supremes never mimed their way through performances or pretended to play instruments, as the Monkees did repeatedly on TV. Transparent about the musical arrangements from the start, the Supremes never needed to make a claim for authenticity like *Headquarters*.

A better claim points to the songwriting of Nesmith, and even the few efforts by Tork and Dolenz. Nesmith wrote some strong material and even minor classics like "Different Drum," "Mary, Mary," or "The Girl I Knew Somewhere." Though Gram Parsons and the Byrds produced earlier and more influential examples of country rock, Nesmith developed enduring examples of that genre as well. Tork's "For Pete's Sake" became the soundtrack to the closing credits on the show's second season. Dolenz's "Randy Scouse Git" received significant airplay for its whimsical and energetic structure and performance. While these cases certainly prove that the Monkees harbored all kinds of talent—in addition to their charismatic and witty acting performances—and measure up to some degree as musical artists, they remain exceptions within and to the whole enterprise. None of the Monkees could produce a "Last Train to Clarksville," "I'm a Believer," or "Daydream Believer."

This defense also collapses in the face of the initial launch of the Monkees and its tremendous immediate success. The argument proves that the Monkees could perform and write their own songs like other bands. It fails to address whether they would meet their own success on their own. How could it prove this point? History already proves otherwise as the whole Monkees media machine delivered on its plan. Proving their individual talent, to whatever scale, fails to address the question of authenticity as it really relates to the vast manipulation of resources and talents beyond the Monkees themselves. As Nik Cohn observed in 1969, it didn't matter whether they had talent. Their own talent was never the point or the question. The system was the talent here.

A shakier argument for the authenticity of the Monkees comes through an old rhetorical move of integrity by association or consecration. These stories usually evoke artists who approve of the Monkees, thereby sanctifying them. Different versions feature John Lennon confessing his love of the show, comparing it to the Marx Brothers, and inviting Nesmith to his pad. George Harrison socialized with Tork, Dolenz with McCartney. The same rhetorical association—a legitimate artist blesses the Monkees, or at least treats them kindly—comes through in noting that Hendrix toured briefly with the Monkees or that Frank Zappa turned up on their TV show. Of course, these stories of saintly associations don't address the real questions of the debate over the authenticity of the Monkees. They merely bypass it, like the question of talent. Whether Lennon or Hendrix enjoyed the Monkees, the approval elides the core issue of who was behind their recordings—their artwork—and how the process was presented to the public. Beyond this deficit in the argument, even the sanctification or extent of it remains unclear. The Beatles, after all, invited many people into their world, most often for some fleeting encounter. No doubt they enjoyed the admiration. We don't know the degree of their confidence in the Monkees. Zappa also relished in any chance to make a mockery of the music biz. His association may carry more of the prankster to it than the peacemaker.

Finally, another rhetorical move involves exploding the authenticity issue. This argument claims that Monkees never hid the machinery and quite flagrantly mocked it from the start. This has merit. But it too bypasses the question of authenticity. It doesn't fail so much in capturing the spirit of the Monkees. Rather it simply remains unpersuasive to the whole crowd raising the issue of authenticity from Richard Goldstein to the curators of the Rock and Roll Hall of Fame. It ignores the historical and social fact that rock developed a culture of appreciation and evaluation wherein authenticity became a significant value. The campy, "Put-On," Pop art irony—laced through the Monkees on the screen and behind the scenes—mocked this value of rock culture. Monkees' fans strain to square their love of their art with this value of authenticity in vain, then. Acknowledging the campiness of the Monkees, as this argument does, recognizes a different set of values (playfulness, anti-seriousness, irony, humor, and liberation), which are almost oppositional to the aesthetics of authenticity.

All these arguments about authenticity are important to understanding the system because a creative industry needs artistic standards and values. It needs critics, formal or informal. Criticism can deepen our understanding of a work and frame our reception of it. Critical values offer tools for articulating how a work resonates with us and why an artist employs formal devices. By the late 1960s, for example, fuzz or distorted amplification could signify rage or explosive liberation. The stark, compressed distortion on John Lennon's *Plastic Ono Band* in this regard, surrounded by sparse instrumentation and often hoarse vocals, signified Lennon's inner turmoil, buried rage, and emotional release. Tactics like these became associated with artistic values of honesty, personal expression, and experimentation (or provocation) in rock culture and criticism of the late 1960s. Rock retained a history of provocation on a social level: Elvis Presley's performances or the blaring volume of "Rock Around the Clock" as blasted out of movie theater speakers in *Blackboard Jungle*. Rock gained a political edge to its provocation in the 1960s with protest songs and its own role in the counterculture. Therefore, provocative formal tactics—piercing distortion, alternative song structures, or abrasive vocal performances, to pick a few examples—were valued. They were seen as authentic expressions of essential elements and values of the genre.

The Monkees' songs offered an uplifting and genuine emotional experience with artful craftsmanship. They could even surprise a classically trained ear like Leonard Bernstein's. Their lack of an origin story, the truths about their formation and production methods, shocked most of the rock critics who operated within the aesthetics described above. But the stories offered up in the arguments for taking this band seriously remain deeply significant for their fans, even if they fail to persuade rock purists. In their efforts to elevate the Monkees to the same high ground as other revered bands, these arguments and stories offer genuine testimony to the meaning devotees find in the artistry of Monkees' productions, both those employing session musicians and those featuring most or all of the Monkees themselves. Even the stories of the band's struggles with Kirshner and with the issue of authenticity itself reflect meaningful values to their fans, touching on their own love of the band's art and the questioning of such appreciation. For thousands of other listeners such debates meant nothing as they knew nothing of them, nothing of the controversy, nothing of the origins of the songs, and only the beauty, vitality, and meaning of the songs themselves—a testimony to the system.

The system—the production and promotion of recorded music—quickly recognized these two worlds of consumers. It then figured out how to tap into the different markets. In other words, the system strategically restructured different parts of its operations, targeting the pre-teen pop market with one set of practices and the adult rock market with another. With a project like *Head*—the film and the album—it became clear that pre-teen bands could not make the transition to this segment of the record-buying public. The Monkees, no matter the quality of the album, lacked the credibility cultivated by this adult-rock, FM-listening, album-cut crowd.

Based on these successes and failures, the system figured out the limits in the market and culture for these different types of acts. It then concentrated on those areas—TV and Top 40 radio, or FM stations and albums—within their respective markets. The Jackson 5, the Partridge Family (a made-for-TV band), Tommy James and the Shondells, or the Banana Splits (yet another kiddie TV band) pursued one part of the market; Jethro Tull, Moby Grape, Led Zeppelin, Joni Mitchell, and James Taylor pursued other parts of the market.

The system responded to the troubles of the Monkees by preserving its overall operations. The system, for all its supportive structure, offered no allegiance to any one act. Each component adhered to its own role and interests. Each component committed to finding and supporting the next hit record for the rewards each—radio, producer, engineer—received for their role in the process. The system even, for this reason, contributed to the Monkees' troubles. To maintain success in a creative economy, where tastes and trends can shift tumultuously, the system's components need to recalibrate with recognized changes in taste or distribution. When FM radio promoted a new format (favoring the allegedly more personal or unconventional expression of album cuts), the programming changes conflicted with the Top 40 emphasis of the Monkees. Their failed late stabs at capturing this new market ("Porpoise Song" and the *Head* campaign) proved them to be behind the times. Moreover, their reputation as a pop TV band hindered their acceptance in this new arena. The systemic role of radio in the industry remained the same: airplay helped sell albums and singles. However, the cultural tastes guiding radio programming shifted. Successful stations and record promotions recognized and harnessed this cultural shift guiding the system.

The specter of authenticity haunted the Monkees even more once they had won some independence, even while their success teetered, untethered from cohesive management. Almost all the important elements of the system that aided the ascendence of the Monkees evolved in different ways by 1967 and 1968. Radio experimented with new formats, itself partially a response to new music trends and ideas about the structure and shape of albums. Their management team splintered, with Raybert's business partners pursuing film production (including an ill-considered Monkees film), while Lester Sill supervised the various producers and songwriters contributing to their dispersed recording sessions. If Nesmith fought to make the Monkees an authentic, coherent band, he also showed a lack of interest in most of the band's endeavors, often skipping out on recording sessions that did not involve his own material.

In this sensing of changing cultural values, the evaluations and standards of gatekeepers changed. Thus, the system that created the Monkees, still in place in the same organizational structure, now gave them trouble. The Monkees' problems in 1968 and 1969, therefore, demonstrate the role that cultural and artistic values play in the system. It's as if the Monkees exposed the machinery of pop, even that behind its most allegedly authentic performers, and exposed why authenticity may not be the real issue at all. They drew attention to the components necessary for any band or musician working in this industry. The Monkees forced admission of the roles played by promoters, publicists, producers, studio musicians, and the media. They brought all the behind-the-scenes machinations of the pop industry to the surface: the genius of the system.

References

Introduction: Machine-Made Monkees

1 "What Goes On?" *Crawdaddy!* (January 1967), p. 14.
2 Richard Goldstein, *Another Little Piece of My Heart: My Life of Rock and Revolution in the '60s* (New York, 2015), p. 119.
3 Thomas Schatz cites and discusses Bazin's notion of the system in the introduction to his *The Genius of the System: Hollywood Filmmaking in the Studio Era* (New York, 1989).
4 See Paul Hirsch, "The Structure of the Popular Music Industry," Survey Research Center, University of Michigan (Ann Arbor, MI, 1969), and Richard A. Peterson and David G. Berger, "Entrepreneurship in Organizations: Evidence from the Popular Music Industry," *Administrative Science Quarterly*, XVI/1 (March 1971), pp. 97–106. The overview of the pop music industry here—as elsewhere in the book—draws heavily from the insights in these two important works.

1 Made in Hollywood

1 Bobby Hart, *Psychedelic Bubble Gum: Boyce and Hart, The Monkees, and Turning Mayhem into Miracles* (New York, 2015).
2 See Cory Messenger, "Record Collectors: Hollywood Record Labels in the 1950s and 1960s," *Media International Australia*, 48 (August 2013), pp. 118–26. Trade paper quotations and RIAA stats from Messenger. On the rise of Warner Bros. Records, see Peter Ames Carlin, *Sonic Boom* (New York, 2021). On Capitol, see Barney Hoskyns, *Capitol Records* (Los Angeles, CA, 2021). On the rise of the Los Angeles music industry in general, you won't find a better source than Barney Hoskyns, *Waiting for the Sun: Strange Days, Weird Scenes, and the Sound of Los Angeles* (New York, 1996).
3 Hoskyns, *Capitol Records*, p. 104.
4 Hoskyns, *Waiting for the Sun*, p. 55.
5 Ibid., p. 51.

6 See Al Casey interview in the "Studio Musicians" section of the documentary *The Wrecking Crew* (dir. Denny Tedesco, 2008).
7 Richard A. Peterson and David G. Berger, "Cycles in Symbol Production: The Case of Popular Music," *American Sociological Review*, XL/2 (April 1975), pp. 158–73.
8 Gillett, *The Sound of the City*, p. 340.
9 Robert Faulkner, *Hollywood Studio Musicians* (New Brunswick, NJ, 2013), p. 7.
10 Ibid., pp. 16 and 188.
11 See testimony in the "Going West" section of Tedesco, dir., *The Wrecking Crew*.
12 See "RCA Studios in the 60s" discussion board on www.gearspace.com.
13 See J. Cogan and W. Clark, *Temples of Sound: Inside the Great Recording Studios* (San Francisco, CA, 2003), and Milton T. Putnam's conference paper "A Thirty-Five Year History and Evolution of the Recording Studio," Audio Engineering Society (May 1980), pp. 1–14.
14 See Putnam, "A Thirty-Five Year History," as well as Cogan and Clark, *Temples of Sound*.
15 Peterson and Berger, "Cycles in Symbol Production," p. 165. See also Edd Routt, James B. McGrath, and Fredric A. Weiss, *The Radio Format Conundrum* (New York, 1978).
16 R. Serge Denisoff, *Tarnished Gold: The Record Industry Revisited* (New Brunswick, NJ, 1986), p. 240.
17 Ben Fong-Torres, *The Hits Just Keep on Coming: The History of Top 40 Radio* (London, 1998), p. 49.
18 Blore in a letter to the *Gavin Report* in 1959, quoted ibid., p. 49.
19 Ron Jacobs, *KHJ: Inside Boss Radio* (Kindle e-book, 2012), p. 15.
20 Ibid., p. 38.
21 Denisoff, *Tarnished Gold*, p. 243.
22 You can hear the real Don Steele on various Internet sites. On YouTube you can find one of his entire programs if you search "93 KHJ The Real Don Steele." You can also catch his patter on the soundtrack to Quentin Tarantino's *Once Upon a Time in Hollywood* (2019).
23 Jacobs's book (KHJ) includes hundreds of internal memos in a voluminous appendix, all unpaginated. From here on in this chapter, all cited memos derive from this source.
24 Paul Hirsch, "The Structure of the Popular Music Industry," Survey Research Center, University of Michigan (Ann Arbor, MI, 1969), pp. 31–3.
25 Ibid., p. 32.
26 Referenced in an internal KHJ memo (May 18, 1967) in Jacobs, KHJ.
27 Denisoff, *Tarnished Gold*, p. 245.

28 Bill Gavin's Record Report no. 627-A, Monday Supplement, December 19, 1966, p. 1 (Rock and Roll Hall of Fame Archives).
29 Hirsch, "The Structure of the Popular Music Industry," p. 32.
30 Greg Prevost, "Man for All Seasons: An Interview with Eminent Studio Engineer Dave Hassinger," *Ugly Things*, 40 (Fall/Winter 2015), pp. 35–42.
31 Hart discusses Hassinger's contributions in Hart, *Psychedelic Bubble Gum*, p. 117.
32 Jacobs, KHJ, p. 82.

2 "Ben Frank's-Types"

1 Alan Hess, *Googie: Fifties Coffee Shop Architecture* (San Francisco, CA, 1985), p. 61.
2 Historic Resources Inventory, State of California, Resources Agency, Department of Parks and Recreation, "Ben Frank's Coffee Shop" (December 1987).
3 Douglas Haskell, *House and Home* (1952), quoted in Hess, *Googie*, p. 62.
4 Domenic Priore, *Riot on Sunset Strip: Rock'n'Roll's Last Stand in Hollywood* (London, 2015), p. 42.
5 Ibid., p. 41.
6 Ibid., p. 43. Priore contains maps of the Strip and Hollywood area. I also consulted documents accompanying the WeHoArts exhibit, "There's Something Happening Here . . . On the Sunset Strip," which ran from October 2016 to May 2017, particularly its map. You can find many reproductions of Zappa's "Freak Out Hot Spots" online. Jeff Gold's *101 Essential Rock Records: The Golden Age of Vinyl from The Beatles to the Sex Pistols* (Berkeley, CA, 2012) features a sharp two-page spread of it (pp. 40–41).
7 Priore, *Riot*, p. 45. See also Chapter 21 in Mike Davis and Jon Wiener, *Set the Night on Fire: L.A. in the Sixties* (London, 2020).
8 Andrew Ligeti, "The Search for Hallowed Ground in the City of Angels: Spatial Empowerment of the Los Angeles Counterculture 1965–1967," MA thesis, California State University at Northridge, 2012, p. 58.
9 David Kamp, "Live at the Whisky," *Vanity Fair* (November 2000), p. 255.
10 Ligeti, "The Search for Hallowed Ground," p. 59.
11 "Find The Monkees (The Audition)," Season 1, Episode 19, NBC Television Network(January 23, 1967).
12 Thankfully and rightfully, most recent books on the Pop art movement discuss and document the role that the Los Angeles art scene played in its almost immediate success. Start with Thomas Crow's monumental

The Long March of Pop (New Haven, CT, and London, 2015), and Cecile Whiting, *Pop L.A.* (Berkeley, CA, 2006); but see also William Hackman, *Out of Sight* (New York, 2015), and Hunter Drohojowska-Philp, *Rebels in Paradise: The Los Angeles Art Scene and the 1960s* (New York, 2011).

13 Max Kozloff, "'Pop Culture,' Metaphysical Disgust, and the New Vulgarians," *Art International*, 7 (March 1962), p. 34.

14 Lucy Lippard, "New York Pop," cited in Blake Gopnik, *Warhol* (New York, 2020), p. 210.

15 Drohojowska-Philp, *Rebels in Paradise*, pp. 73 and 92. See Priore, *Riot on Sunset Strip*, as well.

16 See the Inter-Office Communication memo in the "Memorabilia" section on Volume One of the Rhino DVD collection of *The Monkees* TV show.

17 Ward Sylvester, quoted in Harold Bronson, ed., *Hey, Hey, We're the Monkees* (Los Angeles, CA, 1996).

18 Pilot script, Paul Mazursky Collection, Margaret Herrick Library, AMPAS. An article in the July 14, 1965, edition of the *Hollywood Reporter* notes Jones's association with a TV pilot prepared by Bert Schneider and Bob Rafelson. Biographical background on members of the Monkees, Schneider, and Rafelson culled from the biography files in the General Collection, Margaret Herrick Library (AMPAS), the show's original promotional material, as well as Bronson, *Hey, Hey, We're the Monkees*, and Andrew Sandoval, *The Monkees: The Day-by-Day Story* (Los Angeles, CA, 2021).

19 "Romp! Romp!," *Newsweek* (October 24, 1966), p. 102. The family tree and "ironic twist" quotations spring from an unsigned article titled "Monkees Awarded Two Gold Records," reproduced in the early pages of the unpaginated *Monkees Archives*, vol. I (2016). Next to it resides yet another "Man-Made Monkees" headline (this one from the KRLA Beat).

20 Frank Judge, "TV Magazine," *Detroit News* (January 1–7, 1967), pp. 47–9.

21 See Susan Sontag, "One Culture and the New Sensibility" and "On Camp," in *Against Interpretation* (New York, 1966). The quotation on Beatles art and Pop art comes from her journals located in the UCLA archives, referenced in Howard Hampton's "The Whole World Is Watching," an essay in the booklet accompanying the Criterion edition of *A Hard Day's Night*.

22 See the essays "The Fifth Beatle," "The Peppermint Lounge Revisited," and "The First Tycoon of Teen," in Tom Wolfe, *The Kandy-Kolored Tangerine-Flake Streamline Baby* (New York, 1965). In the introduction Wolfe describes his subjects as belonging to a "Pop society."

23 "The New Sentimentality," *Esquire* (March 1964), p. 27.

3 The Genius of the System

1 Allan J. Scott, "A Perspective of Economic Geography," *Journal of Economic Geography*, IV/5 (2004), pp. 479–99 (p. 487). See also Scott's *On Hollywood: The Place, the Industry* (Princeton, NJ, 2005).

2 The overview of the music industry in this chapter draws heavily on Paul Hirsch, "The Structure of the Popular Music Industry," Survey Research Center, University of Michigan (Ann Arbor, MI, 1969), and Richard A. Peterson and David G. Berger, "Entrepreneurship in Organizations: Evidence from the Popular Music Industry," *Administrative Science Quarterly*, XVI/1 (March 1971), pp. 97–106, even when not specifically cited.

3 Hirsch, "The Structure of the Popular Music Industry," p. 25. See "Band Battles Trigger Spurts on Instruments," *Billboard* (July 1, 1967), p. 1.

4 Narrative drawn from Johnny Rogan, *Timeless Flight: The Definitive Biography of The Byrds* (London, 1990), primarily Chapter One, and liner notes on the album *Preflyte*. Like Monkees' fans, Byrds' fans get quite defensive about their early history and the use of session musicians, noting that the Byrds took over instrumental chores on their first album.

5 The overview of Kirshner's career draws on Greg Shaw, "Brill Building Pop," in *The Rolling Stone Illustrated History of Rock and Roll*, ed. Anthony DeCurtis and James Henke (New York, 1992), pp. 143–53, and Rich Podolsky, *Don Kirshner: The Man with the Golden Ear* (Milwaukee, WI, 2012).

6 Agreement between Aldon Music, Inc. and Jack Keller, November 5, 1959. Shared with the author by Jordan Keller.

7 See David Suisman, *Selling Sounds: The Commercial Revolution in American Music* (Cambridge, MA, 2009), on the formation of publishing companies and their business practices.

8 King and Hart discuss Kirshner's list making and his methodical approach in their respective autobiographies. See Carole King, *A Natural Woman* (New York, 2012), and Bobby Hart, *Psychedelic Bubble Gum: Boyce and Hart, The Monkees, and Turning Mayhem into Miracles* (New York, 2015).

9 John Rosica, "Patterns in Promotion," a speech before RCA Victor regional distributors, April 27, 1967, quoted in Hirsch, "The Structure of the Popular Music Industry," p. 43.

10 List drawn from promotional material for the Monkees' *Head* (1968) providing RCA's regional outposts. *Cash Box* regularly featured regional

listings of distributors as well, which corroborated this list. Jim Roan at the Smithsonian Institution helped me track down some of the various distributors' catalogs. As Gillett notes in his 1970 history of rock, independent firms lacked a major label's large resources for such thorough and speedy distribution. See Charlie Gillett, *The Sound of the City: The Rise of Rock and Roll* (New York, 1970), p. 341.

4 State-of-the-Art Song System

1 Hart tells this story in Bobby Hart, *Psychedelic Bubble Gum: Boyce and Hart, The Monkees, and Turning Mayhem into Miracles* (New York, 2015), Chapter 20 ("Something About a Train to Somewhere").
2 *Inside Pop: The Rock Revolution*, CBS Television Network, broadcast April 25, 1967.
3 Thomas Brothers, *Help!: The Beatles, Duke Ellington and the Magic of Collaboration* (New York, 2019), pp. xi–xv.
4 You can find this anecdote in any number of stories – and there are many! – about the creation of this song.
5 Paul Hirsch, "The Structure of the Popular Music Industry," Survey Research Center, University of Michigan (Ann Arbor, MI, 1969), p. 39.
6 Jesse Burt and Bob Ferguson, *So You Want to Be in Music!* (Nashville, TN, 1970), p. 85.

5 Air Guitar

1 From a TV *Guide* article quoted in Andrew Sandoval, *The Monkees: The Day-by-Day Story* (Los Angeles, CA, 2021), p. 126.
2 Monkees folder, General Collection, Margaret Herrick Library, AMPAS.
3 See Ward Sylvester's testimony on this service in Harold Bronson, *Hey, Hey, We're the Monkees* (Los Angeles, CA, 1996), p. 22. See also Miles Beller, "How Networks Test for Audience Impact," *New York Times* (June 3, 1979).
4 Nik Cohn, *Awopbopaloobop Alopbamboom: The Golden Age of Rock* (New York, 1996), p. 216.
5 Promotional material reproduced in *Monkees Archives, Vol. 2* (2016), unpaginated.
6 Richard Neupert, *A History of the French New Wave Cinema* (Madison, WI, 2007), p. xi.
7 First draft, August 17, 1965, "The Monkeys [*sic*] Pilot," Paul Mazursky Collection, Margaret Herrick Library.
8 "Synthetic Quartet Will Hit Tube Hard," *Washington Post* (May 31, 1966).

9 Quoted in Sandoval, *The Monkees*, p. 235.
10 Jack Gould, "The Monkees," *New York Times* (September 13, 1966).
11 Quoted in Bronson, *Hey, Hey, We're the Monkees*, p. 108.
12 Quoted in Sandoval, *The Monkees*, p. 234 (January 21, 1967).
13 "10 'HQ' Tunes in Monkees Rerun," *Billboard* (June 3, 1967), p. 10.
14 Monkees folder, General Collection, Margaret Herrick Library.
15 "Kirshner Focus of Rumors," *Record World* (March 18, 1967), pp. 3–4. The article goes on to note "recent gossip column items concerning discontent of the Monkees with one another," their "well-known" lack of musicianship and songwriting, and conflicts within management.

6 A Quartered Head

1 Like many myths, even true ones, this story gets repeated endlessly and you can find it in all kinds of different sources. Andrew Sandoval discovered depositions for a 1967 court case related to these events offering robust testimony to the meeting. He reproduces some of them in the latest edition of *The Monkees: The Day-by-Day Story* (Los Angeles, CA, 2021), pp. 243–5.
2 Court papers quoted in "Kirshner and Col-SG Collide—He Sues," *Billboard* (March 25, 1967), p. 3.
3 Ibid., p. 4.
4 Quoted in Andrew Sandoval, *The Monkees: The Day-by-Day Story* (San Diego, CA, 2005), p. 143. For more details, see David Finkle, "Monkees Dispute: Kirshner Sues For $35,500,000," *Record World* (March 25, 1967), p. 3.
5 Michael Cable, *The Pop Industry Inside Out* (London, 1977), p. 47.
6 Bob Stanley, *Yeah! Yeah! Yeah!* (New York, 2014), p. 207.
7 Lester Sill on the *Headquarters* radio show in 1988. Cited in Jim Catapano, "Anarchy in LA: An Act of Rock'n' Roll Rebellion Preserves a Legacy," *Monkees Live Almanac* (March 12, 2016), www.monkeeslivealmanac.com.
8 Quoted in Sandoval, *The Monkees*, p. 118.
9 Quoted in Harold Bronson, *Hey, Hey, We're the Monkees* (Los Angeles, 1996), p. 147.
10 Promotional material reproduced in *Monkees Archives, Vol. 2*, unpaginated.
11 "The Screen: 'Head,' Monkees Move for a Turned-On Audience," *New York Times* (November 7, 1968), p. 37.
12 *Amusement Business* (October 1969), quoted in Sandoval, *The Monkees*, p. 253.

13 Tom Donahue, "AM Radio: 'Stinking Up the Airways'," originally published in *Rolling Stone* on November 23, 1967, collected in *The Rolling Stone Reader*, ed. Ben Fong-Torres (New York, 1974), pp. 672–6.
14 "KMPX-FM's Donahue Programs Music with a Wide Open View," *Billboard* (December 30, 1967), p. 18.
15 Alfred G. Aronowitz, "Was the Pop Music of the 1960s the Most? Or Just a Mess?" *Saturday Evening Post* (July 15, 1967).
16 Promotional material reproduced in *Monkees Archives, Vol. 2*.
17 Bill Gavin's Record Report no. 613-B, Wednesday Supplement (September 14, 1966), p. 1(Rock and Roll Hall of Fame Archives).
18 *Pop Chronicles*, Episode 44: "Revolt of the Fat Angel" (Part 4), UNT Digital Library, University of North Texas Libraries, www.digital.library.unt.edu.
19 Ann Moses, *Meow! My Groovy Life with Tiger Beat's Teen Idols* (Seattle, WA, 2017), p. 70.

Select Bibliography

Archives

Dee Caruso Papers, Writers Guild of America, Los Angeles, CA
Gavin Report Collection, Rock and Roll Hall of Fame, Cleveland, OH
Paul Mazursky Collection, Margaret Herrick Library, Academy of Motion Pictures and Sciences (AMPAS), Beverly Hills, CA

Web Archives

John Gilliland's *Pop Chronicles*, www.digital.library.unt.edu
KRLA *Beat*, www.krlabeat.sakionline.net
Rock's Backpages, www.rocksbackpages.com
Sunshine Factory (Monkees fan site), www.monkees.coolcherrycream.com
World Radio History, worldradiohistory.com

Documentaries

Tedesco, Denny, dir., *The Wrecking Crew* (2008)

Articles and Books

Anon., *Monkees Archives*, 3 vols (West Chester, PA, 2016)

Anon., KRLA *Chronological Archives*, 6 vols (West Chester, PA, 2016)

Barker, Hugh, and Yuval Taylor, *Faking It: The Quest for Authenticity in Popular Music* (New York, 2002)

Basirico, Laurence Albert, "Stickin' Together: The Cohesiveness of Rock Groups," MA thesis, State University of New York at Stony Brook, 1974

Becker, Howard S., *Art Worlds* (Berkeley, CA, 1982)

Bovey, Seth, *Five Years Ahead of My Time: Garage Rock from the 1950s to the Present* (London, 2019)

Boyce, Tommy, *How to Write a Hit Song . . . and Sell It* (Hollywood, CA, 1975)

Brothers, Thomas, *Help! The Beatles, Duke Ellington and the Magic of Collaboration* (New York, 2019)

Burt, Jesse, with Bob Ferguson, *So You Want to Be in Music!* (Nashville, TN, 1970)

Caves, Richard E., *Creative Industries: Contracts Between Art and Commerce* (Cambridge MA, 2000)

Cogan, Jim, and William Clark, *Temples of Sound: Inside the Great Recording Studios* (San Francisco, CA, 2003)

Cohn, Nik, *Awopbopaloobop Alopbamboom: The Golden Age of Rock* (New York, 1996)

Crow, Thomas, *The Long March of Pop* (New Haven, CT, and London, 2015)

Davis, Mike, and Jon Wiener, *Set the Night on Fire: L.A. in the Sixties* (London, 2020)

Denisoff, R. Serge, *Tarnished Gold: The Record Industry Revisited* (New Brunswick, NJ, 1986)

Douglas, Susan, *Listening In: Radio and the American Imagination* (New York, 1999)

Draper, Robert, *Rolling Stone Magazine: The Uncensored Story* (New York, 1990)

Drohojowska-Philp, Hunter, *Rebels in Paradise: The Los Angeles Art Scene and the 1960s* (New York, 2011)

Emerson, Ken, *Always Magic in the Air: The Bomp and Brilliance of the Brill Building Era* (New York, 2005)

Fatherley, Richard W., and David T. MacFarland, *The Birth of Top 40 Radio: The Storz Stations' Revolution of the 1950s and 1960s* (Jefferson, NC, 2014)

Faulkner, Robert R., *Hollywood Studio Musicians* (New Brunswick, NJ, 2013)

Fisher, Marc, *Something in the Air: Radio, Rock, and the Revolution that Shaped a Generation* (New York, 2007)

Fong-Torres, Ben, *The Hits Just Keep on Coming: The History of Top 40 Radio* (London, 1998)

Gillett, Charlie, *The Sound of the City: The Rise of Rock and Roll* (New York, 1970)

Goldstein, Richard, *Another Little Piece of My Heart: My Life of Rock and Revolution in the '60s* (New York, 2015)

Hackman, William, *Out of Sight: The Los Angeles Art Scene of the Sixties* (New York, 2015)

Hagan, Joe, *Sticky Fingers: The Life and Times of Jann Wenner and Rolling Stone Magazine* (New York, 2017)

Hart, Bobby, *Psychedelic Bubble Gum: Boyce and Hart, The Monkees, and Turning Mayhem into Miracles* (New York, 2015)
Hartman, Kent, *The Wrecking Crew* (New York, 2012)
Hirsch, Paul, "The Structure of the Popular Music Industry," Survey Research Center, University of Michigan (Ann Arbor, MI, 1969)
—, "Processing Fads and Fashions: An Organization-Set Analysis of Cultural Industry Systems," *American Journal of Sociology*, LXXVII/4 (January 1972), pp. 639–59
Hoskyns, Barney, *Waiting for the Sun: Strange Days, Weird Scenes, and the Sound of Los Angeles* (New York, 1996)
Jacobs, Ron, *KHJ: Inside Boss Radio* (Kindle e-book, 2012)
King, Carole, *A Natural Woman* (New York, 2012)
Ligeti, Andrew, "The Search for Hallowed Ground in the City of Angels: Spatial Empowerment of the Los Angeles Counterculture 1965–1967," MA thesis, California State University at Northridge, 2012
Mabey, Richard, *The Pop Process* (London, 1969)
Melly, George, *Revolt into Style: The Pop Arts* (New York, 1971)
Meltzer, Richard, *The Aesthetics of Rock* (New York, 1970)
Messenger, Cory "Record Collectors: Hollywood Record Labels in the 1950s and 1960s," *Media International Australia*, 48 (August 2013), pp. 118–26
Nesmith, Michael, *Infinite Tuesday: An Autobiographical Riff* (New York, 2018)
Neupert, Richard, *A History of the French New Wave Cinema* (Madison, WI, 2007)
Peterson, Richard A., and David G. Berger, "Entrepreneurship in Organizations: Evidence from the Popular Music Industry," *Administrative Science Quarterly*, XVI/1 (March 1971), pp. 97–106
Podolsky, Rich *Don Kirshner: The Man with the Golden Ear* (Milwaukee, WI, 2012)
Powers, Devon, *Writing the Record: The Village Voice and the Birth of Rock Criticism* (Amherst, MA, 2013)
Priore, Domenic, *Riot on Sunset Strip: Rock'n'Roll's Last Stand in Hollywood* (London, 2007)
Putnam, Milton T., "Recording Studio and Control Room Facilities of Advance Design," *Journal of the Audio Engineering Society*, VIII/2 (April 1960), pp. 111–19
—, "A Thirty-Five-Year History and Evolution of the Recording Studio," *Audio Engineering Reprint*, paper presented at the 66th Convention of the Audio Engineering Society, May 6–9, 1980, Los Angeles, CA

Reilly, Edward, with Maggie McManus and William Chadwick, *The Monkees: A Manufactured Image; The Ultimate Reference Guide to Monkee Memories and Memorabilia* (Ann Arbor, MI, 1987)

Riley, Tim, *Tell Me Why: The Beatles; Album by Album, Song by Song, the Sixties and After* (New York, 1988)

Rogan, Johnny, *Timeless Flight: The Definitive Biography of the Byrds* (London, 1990)

Sandoval, Andrew, *The Monkees: The Day-by-Day Story* (San Diego, CA, 2005)

—, *The Monkees: The Day-by-Day Story* (Los Angeles, CA, 2021)

Scott, Allen J., *On Hollywood: The Place, the Industry* (Princeton, NJ, 2005)

Shaw, Greg, "Brill Building Pop," in *The Rolling Stone Illustrated History of Rock and Roll*, ed. Anthony DeCurtis and James Henke (New York, 1992), pp. 143–53

Shemel, Sidney, and M. William Krasilovsky, *This Business of Music* (New York, 1964)

Simpson, Kim, *Early '70s Radio: The American Format Revolution* (New York, 2011)

Suisman, David, *Selling Sounds: The Commercial Revolution in American Music* (Cambridge, MA, 2009)

Whiting, Cecile, *Pop L.A.* (Berkeley, CA, 2006)

Discography

The Monkees
(Colgems COM/COS 101)

More of the Monkees
(Colgems COM/COS 102)

Headquarters
(Colgems COM/COS 103)

Pisces, Aquarius, Capricorn & Jones Ltd.
(Colgems COM/COS 104)

The Birds, the Bees, and the Monkees
(Colgems COM/COS 109)

Head
(Colgems COSO 5008)

Acknowledgments

Apropos of the book's theme, I thank from the depths of my heart a whole support structure of people. My family tolerated my distractions and dinner conversations and gave me company while we listened to records. I relish talking music with the loves of my life, my sons Jack and Dash, at the dinner table (sometimes, understandably, when the talk turned too esoteric, their beautiful mother banned such discussions). It moves me to my core to share such dialogues with them in this way. Great friends like Danny and Casey listened to me air out ideas. Archivists tracked down material and answered questions; scholars and insiders answered even more questions and offered feedback; the whole Reaktion team carried my work forward. No genius on my end, just a robust and enriching system of support.

My lifelong friend Danny Korobkin (and high school bandmate) talked about the ideas here over and over again with me. These discussions reel back to our teen years, and then, as now, I stood in awe of Danny's intelligence, probing imagination, insights, and wit. He's always been a hero of mine. I truly treasure our friendship.

I owe Jenn Kozicki and Max Liszt for a timely invite to our family to go on a camping trip and for taking care of Alison and Dash while I stayed home to finish a draft with a weekend deadline.

I thank the incredible and instructive staff at Record Surplus ("the last record store") for their essential work, the joy they bring to my life, and their warm reception whenever I bring my whole family there. I thank Monkees' fans for all of their websites and collections, and their passion and dedication. Biggest props of all in this regard goes to Andrew Sandoval and his respect for the importance of archival documentation on top of his fandom. I thank him for a delightful chat and for sharing insights and perspectives derived from his own rigorous writing and research (I also thank Josh Kun for helping to arrange this meeting). I appreciate Robert Faulkner for his correspondence with me on his work on studio musicians in 1960s

Los Angeles. I am so grateful to Paul Hirsch for our email exchanges on the 1960s music business and his stellar early sociological study, a strong foundation for my work here. In turn, I was honored that he read an early draft of this book, offering sharp tips for improvement and his endorsement. My intrepid and dear friend Dana Polan, as always, read an early draft and showered it with suggestions and support. Michael St. Pierre and Alex Klyce generously read the manuscript, offering crucial commentary and spirited conversation. Jordan Keller read a few chapters, answered questions about his dad's work with Kirshner and the Monkees, shared key contracts, pictures, and documents with me, and helped with his professional perspective on issues like royalty structures and contracts. I'll always remember our correspondence and conversation. A serendipitous encounter with David Hesmondhalgh (at a Parisian cafe, no less) led to the good fortune of my meeting this engaging scholar and person, and also to his considerate reading of a few early chapter drafts. My piano and music theory teacher David Naffie read and discussed my analysis of the songs, as did Danny Korobkin, who carefully, thoughtfully, rigorously, and passionately walked me through the music, like the true friend (and fellow fan) that he is. They helped me avoid making foolish claims about the music. Any that remain, of course, belong to me alone. I play the fool better than any instrument. Huge thanks to Barney Hoskyns for writing the best critical and historical book on southern California's music scene and for his heroic Internet archive *Rock's Backpages*.

Finally, my soulmate, Alison. We've been on a long road together and a long road stretches out ahead of us. At the very start of this project, on a brilliant Santa Barbara hike one day, with her encouragement, she generously listened to me map out the book as I wound my way through every chapter on our trek. Later, she read every chapter and came up with a twist and a fix for the order of the first two. We've shared so much: school, love, children, parenting, ideas, food, hikes, music, family, friends. She restructured this book and years ago restructured my life. I only feel grace and gratitude for her intellectual and spiritual light and the music we make of our life together. Having such a partner is beyond dreams and belief. This one is for her.

Photo Acknowledgments

The authors and publishers wish to thank the relevant organizations and individuals listed below for authorizing reproduction of their work.

Author's collection: pp. 19, 32, 38, 40, 49, 51, 57, 75 left and right, 102 (shared with author by Jordan Keller), 105, 134, 135, 142, 147, 164, 165, 174, 176; Sebastian Ballard: pp. 6, 31; Getty Images: pp. 21 (Michael Ochs Archives), 68 (Steve Schapiro), 72 (Bettmann), 97 (Michael Ochs Archives), 101 (The Estate of David Gahr), 114 (Michael Ochs Archives), 149 (NBC Television), 153 (Keystone Features), 156 (Richard Weize), 172 (Michael Ochs Archives); Shutterstock Editorial: p. 59 (George Brich/AP); Wikimedia Commons: p. 117 (public domain).

Index

Page numbers in *italics* indicate illustrations